ADVAN
<u>**THE TRAJECTORY OF CHANGE**</u>

"In the clearest of language, Michael Albert lays bare the weaknesses of the left and points to the opportunities ahead. Eschewing cynicism and defeatism, he outlines positive alternatives that will attract and retain social activists, and, most importantly, achieve tangible victories. If you're tired of complaining about the ills of capitalism and ready to articulate what we want and how to get there, read this book."

—Medea Benjamin, founding director of Global Exchange

"Written in an accessible manner and profoundly thought-provoking, this book helps us to remember that a movement of resistance to oppression is essential; a movement with vision and strategy is compelling."

—Bill Fletcher, national organizer for the Black Radical Congress

"Cross global activism with common sense, and you get Michael Albert's new book. It's clear, useful, and short. You will not agree with all of his suggestions, but this book will start you thinking: What *would* work? How *do* we solve the real problems of our movement?"

—Mike Prokosch, coordinator of the global economy program at United for a Fair Economy

"I read Michael Albert's book with great interest. Like Albert, I think we will be able to challenge capitalism only if we can create an international movement that retains and empowers its members. If I am soon jailed in my home country, France, I will use the time to read again *The Trajectory of Change* and to take advantage of my forced rest to elaborate on its new strategies. I hope others will do likewise."

—José Bové, author of *The World Is Not for Sale*

THE TRAJECTORY
OF CHANGE

ACTIVIST STRATEGIES
FOR SOCIAL TRANSFORMATION

Michael Albert

SOUTH END PRESS
CAMBRIDGE, MASSACHUSETTS

Cover design by Ellen P. Shapiro
Cover photo at World Economic Forum protest in New
    York, February 2, 2002, by Eric Ruder/*Socialist Worker*.
Union printed in Canada. First printing.

Library of Congress Cataloging-in-Publication Data

Albert, Michael, 1947–
    The trajectory of change : activist strategies for social
transformation / Michael Albert.
        p. cm.
    Includes bibliographical references and index.
    ISBN 0-89608-662-3 (paper : alk. paper) — ISBN
0-89608-663-1 (cloth : alk. Paper)
        1. Social movements—United States. 2. Social
change—United States. 3. Political activists—United States.
4. Right and left (Political science) I. Title

HN65 .A67 2002
303.48'4'0973—dc21

                                                    2002018711

            South End Press, 7 Brookline Street, #1
                Cambridge, MA 02139-4146
                    www.southendpress.org
                    Printed in Canada

    06 05 04 03 02   1 2 3 4 5

TABLE OF CONTENTS

ACKNOWLEDGMENTS

The material in this book first appeared in various essays in *Z Magazine* or the on-line ZNet web site (http://www.zmag.org). In those incarnations, the essays received direct editing input from Eric Sargent and Lydia Sargent. In addition, I often send articles I prepare to various friends — Robin Hahnel, Stephen Shalom, Cynthia Peters, and Noam Chomsky in particular — for comment. That likely happened with earlier versions of this material, and so their excellent explicit suggestions are embodied, for which I thank them.

Beyond that, the material here obviously arises from my experience in diverse movements. The insights are wisdom from those movements. Any less-than-wise content is a misperception of their history. The movements are the true author of this volume. For the misperceptions, as translator, my apologies.

This book came about at the suggestion of South End Press when, at the time of the anti-globalization activism of early 2001, a particular essay, the "Trajectory of Change," struck a chord. The suggestion arose for a short volume of material regarding the prospects and possibilities of current movements. This book would not exist but for that request. My reply to the request was to provide a rather amorphous collection of essays to South End's Anthony Arnove, who took charge of the project. He selected from that collection pieces out of which to mold this book. He gave the pieces order, eliminated poor presentation, edited poor locutions, and generally made this a very succinct and accessible book rather than a mere selection of disconnected essays. He did all this far more adroitly than I would have and, indeed, I think my best decision regarding this volume was to fully follow his lead.

FOREWORD

WHAT'S DIFFERENT, WHAT'S THE SAME, WHAT DO WE DO?

With the exception of this foreword and an afterward, the material in this book was all written well before September 11, 2001. When I received the manuscript back for final adjustment in early November 2001, not having seen the manuscript since mid-summer, there was an obvious question.

The U.S. was not at war when the manuscript was written. It is at war now. How does the book contribute to that new context? Did I need to update each section in some dramatic fashion, or even update it at all?

My answer was no.

But how could I think that a book written about activism and movement strategy before 9/11 could retain relevance in the period after 9/11? Hadn't the world profoundly altered and the overall context of activism changed fundamentally? Wouldn't that necessitate a rewrite?

The thing is, I don't think there has been such a change. The basic institutions of our societies are the same now as they were before 9/11. Capitalist ownership relations, corporate divisions of labor, markets, bourgeois states with their various party arrangements, obedient mass media, nuclear families, and cultural communities often at hostile odds with one another. These are still the context in which we act.

The basic logic of dissent is also unchanged since 9/11. We choose issues to better the lot of suffering constituencies and to simultaneously increase prospects for more gains in the future. Short term, we raise social costs until elites agree to implement our demands or end policies we oppose. Longer term, we accumulate support and develop movement infrastructure and alternative institutions, while working toward transforming society's defining relations.

Before 9/11 and now, too — and in the future as well, no doubt — basic constituencies to organize derive from ownership relations, divisions of labor, cultural community allegiances, gender roles, and sexual preferences.

So what's different?

We are at war. Or rather we are bombing rubble into ash while starving a country's population.

Foreword

As I write this foreword, the U.S. is pursuing policies that could kill a million or more people in the next few months. Of course, this places a huge immediate responsibility on us to act to stop the carnage. Hopefully our efforts and those of activists around the world will have aided Afghan's citizens by the time you read this. Hopefully the immediate proximate war will be over, in part due to inspired resistance. If not, or even if so, the lessons in this volume should aid in anti-war work, just as in anti-globalization work, just as in anti-racist work, and so on.

While bombing, Bush, Blair, and Co. are also using fear and anger to ram home draconian and redistributive legislation, precisely in the same manner as was done throughout the Cold War, but much faster. The scale of their hypocritical venality is awesome, and this requires our activist attention, as well.

So we must relate to the immediate and more long-term "war on terrorism" and its correlated new elite priorities, but there is some understandable debate about how. Do we drop everything else? What can we usefully do to end this war and reverse draconian and redistributive government attacks on working people?

The answer, as I write in mid-November, is that we can seek to greatly enlarge dissent and to give it a character that communicates to ruling elements: if you don't stop your war, the price you will pay will be more than you are willing to bear.

But how can we impose such a price on our governments and the constituencies they serve?

History suggests that we have trouble addressing this question. Some of us think when we reveal to elites the scope of their policy's injustice, their own moral qualms will move them. Some of us think that high numbers with high militancy seeking peace is needed. But the truth is that Bush and Blair and Co. have no morals and can weather any small storm. What really catches their attention and can turn their priorities upside down is the threat of movements that not only increasingly oppose today's war, but move on to oppose, as well, other instances of injustice, and, most threateningly, the basic conditions that breed injustice.

Warmakers make war not because they are sadists who love war, but to defend and enhance their position and power. They think twice about making war not because they get upset about the body count, and not because they are embarrassed by the size of opposition, but only when movements provoked by their war start to threaten the warmakers' underlying position and power. Warmakers think twice, that is, when they realize that pursuing war has the opposite of their intended effect. Instead of serving their position and power, their war cuts their own throats. Then and only then, all things considered, they become inclined to stop. Many factors contribute, including instability and opposition abroad, and our own activism in the United States.

The point is, even for U.S. activists who have no other priority than to stop the war, the current situation calls not for ignoring all other issues and speaking only of war, and certainly not for toning down dissent, but for as many people as possible to be as visibly active and energetic at they are able to be, developing as broad a set of linkages between war opposition and other oppositions as they can possibly generate.

The current situation doesn't entreat that those who are anti-corporate, anti-globalization, anti–death penalty, anti-racist, anti–tax ripoffs, or anti–undemocratic elections shelve such focuses and become only anti-war. Quite the contrary, it entreats that all these folks, and others with prior progressive commitments, be more aggressively anti-corporate and all the rest, even as we also increase our efforts to oppose the war. It entreats us to try to respectfully bring as many people who are becoming anti-war, anti-starvation, anti–foreign policy debacle, anti–what have you as possible into also becoming anti-corporate and so on, and vice-versa, since attaining that kind of mutuality is precisely the trajectory of growing solidarity and diversifying focus that will most effectively compel a change in the war and in other issues, as well.

So what is different since 9/11 is not the ultimate focus of dissent, logic of dissent, or aim of dissent? What has significantly changed is instead:

(i) the immediate urgency of dissent specifically against the war and bombing, since the lives of millions of potentially starved souls are directly at stake;

(ii) some additional focuses of dissent including the draconian surveillance and other legislation and the hypocritical "stimulus" boondoggle for the rich; and

(iii) the prospects for dissent, since, despite flag waving patriotic media, way more people than before 9/11 are now seriously open to discuss world affairs and activism.

In other words, this is a time for fighting against this war in order to save innumerable lives, as well as to prevent catastrophes of even greater proportion beyond Afghanistan. But it is also a time for reasserting our existing focuses and struggles. We should not be running from our earlier progressive priorities nor even just pausing them. We need to enlarge our ongoing efforts and to link them to the anti-war effort. That will enhance all our prospects, anti-war and others, as well.

Is there a practical implication of all this that goes beyond urging the multi-issue mindset we should each individually embrace? I think we need a new Peace and Justice Coalition.

Peace should mean no war, no imposed biological and chemical starvation, no mass policies of assault on populations, plus legal pursuit of and prosecution of all terrorists.

Justice should mean rewriting the rules of economic and social exchange to redistribute power and income from the rich to the poor, and this should be so whether we are talking about international trade and globalization or about domestic stimulus and other policy.

Current U.S. policies could starve to death a million people in the next few months while simultaneously inducing all manner of reactionary trends in countries around the world, as well as here at home. Surely we can envision the possible human consequences of all this sufficiently to galvanize our attention.

This is a time to fight war by whatever channels we can work through and to create a multi-issue, multi-tactic, popular, mass movement that sets aside squabbles for solidarity and that dispenses with doctrinaire ideology for plain talking and well-thought-out vision, program, and strategy.

And this is a book about doing precisely that, which therefore retains its relevance post–9/11.

THE TRAJECTORY OF CHANGE

From the demonstrations in Seattle through Prague and Quebec, the left has organized an opposition that is steadfast and strong, and which is raising havoc with the masters' plans to further enrich and empower the already rich and powerful. Yet, we have also established an activist style that could plateau well short of what's needed to win change. We need some mid-course correction.

What's the problem with our activist style? After all, thousands of militant, courageous people are turning out in city after city. They are opposing globalization and they are even beginning to oppose corporate power more broadly. Aren't the minions of money on the run? Isn't the horrible impact of the WTO, IMF, World Bank, and now also the Free Trade Area of the Americas (FTAA) revealed for all to see? Isn't profit-making itself coming under fire? Isn't this becoming the best time for activism in decades?

Yes, this is all happening, with youth pushing the project, and energies climbing. But our goal is not only to do better than in past years, but to win changes that improve millions of lives. To win "non-reformist reforms" that will take us toward comprehensive justice requires strategic thinking.

But isn't that what's been happening? Aren't we strategizing about these big events and successfully implementing our plans, even against extensive police opposition? Yes. But we want to prevent horrible trade agreements, to end the IMF and World Bank, and to then win new global and domestic institutions. To do all that requires ever-widening support with ever-growing political comprehension. We need massive movements that combine multiple tactics to raise social costs that elites can't bear and to which they ultimately give in. We need to expand our movements in size and diversify them in focus and tactics until elites meet our current demands — and then we need to go for more.

From Seattle on, steadily more people and ever-wider constituencies should have joined our anti-globalization (and other) movements. Our activities should have continued to highlight large events when doing so was appropriate for building our movements, of course, but they should also have emphasized more regional and local organizing, in smaller cities and towns, reaching people unable to travel around the world to Los Angeles, Prague, Quebec, or wherever else. Folks are working creatively on all this, to be sure, but they need more help and these trends need greater respect and support.

For all the wonderful successes of recent times, still, given the immensity of our aims, we have to ask: why aren't our numbers growing quite as much as we'd like? Why aren't new constituencies joining the project quite as fast as we would like them to? Why aren't the venues of activism diversifying still more quickly to local sites as well as massive focal points?

Part of the answer is that progress, after all, takes time. Movement building is not easy. Another part of the answer is that, in fact, we have experienced some rapid growth. For example, the proliferation of Indy Media Centers provides alternative local news and analysis that interactively span nearly 40 cities in 15 countries, a virtually unprecedented achievement. But Indy Media growth occurs by refining the involvement of people already largely committed. That's wonderful, but it is internal solidification, not outward enlargement.

Similarly, we have witnessed the impressive and steadily improving preparation, creativity, knowledge, and courage among those who have been demonstrating. Consider the reports about the youthful anarchists and other militants street fighting in Quebec. Unlike in Seattle, I heard repeatedly about their solidarity with others, their defending others, their courage and discipline, and the support they garnered. This is tremendous progress. Would that all other parts of our left learned and adapted their choices as fast as these most militant young folks have been doing. But this, too, occurs not based on wide outreach, but by manifesting steadily increasing insights and connections among those who are already highly involved.

As for outreach, we have to face the fact that from Seattle right through Quebec, the size of our demonstrations has not grown much at all. Let me try an admittedly exaggerated, even Olympian, but hopefully fitting analogy to illustrate my point. Imagine a marathon race. As thousands of runners burst out at the start, folks are bunched in a huge moving mass. Yet, however entwined they are at the outset, each competes with all others. The faster runners want to escape the impact of the huge mass. They break off and speed up, creating a gap between themselves and the mass now lagging behind.

In time, inside this fast group, too, there is uneven development. Some runners are having a better day. Before long, they open a second gap, now between themselves and the large leading group they have been part of, and they extend that gap sufficiently to break contact. Those left behind lose momentum for want of connection with the inspiring fastest runners, just as happened with the more massive pack earlier. Eventually, a final breakaway happens, with the few who will compete down the stretch leaving behind the already tiny lead pack, the bigger pack behind that, and the mass lagging way out of sight.

Like a marathon, movement struggle goes a long distance, requires endurance, and has to overcome obstacles. A big population is involved and we would, of course, like to succeed as quickly as possible. Speed of attaining our ultimate ends matters greatly and even reaching secondary aims like ending a war, abolishing the IMF, raising wages, or winning a shorter work day is better if achieved sooner than later. Yet winning social change is in other respects not like a typical race — or it shouldn't be, at any rate.

With social change, the winning logic shouldn't be for those who develop unequally and are "faster" to leave the slower pack behind and cross a finish line first. The only way to win the "social change race" is for the whole pack to cross all together and as fast as this whole can be induced to go. The fastest and otherwise best activists need to stay with the pack, working to increase its speed as a whole, even if it means holding themselves back a bit at times. A little spread between the more advanced and the rest, taking the form of exemplary activity, may sometimes be excellent, of course, but not at too great a spread.

Our social change effort should actually be more like a large group trying to scale a huge mountain. Imagine watching such a group and seeing the best prepared or stronger or more committed climbers rush out way in advance of the rest, so far as to cut the connection, neither helping the other any longer. The self-defeating nature of that choice would be self-evident. But that is our current problem as I see it. We have a partial disconnection between many of our most informed activists and the bulk of people who are dissatisfied with the status quo but inactive or just beginning to become active.

This disconnection induces some to become ever more highly involved and to interact fantastically well with one another, even having their own supportive subculture, but to simultaneously lose touch with others who then become long-distance spectators, watching the lead pack (vulnerably) power off into the distance, detached from it. I am not saying this is a done deal. But I think it is an emerging difficulty we need to address.

I speak every so often at college campuses where the division I am trying to convey is easy to see. As compared to their schoolmates, the activists look entirely different, have different tastes and preferences, talk differently, and are largely insulated from rather than immersed in the larger population. The situation exists in other communities, as well.

Lots of factors contribute to this disconnection. None are easy to precisely identify, much less correct. Nonetheless, one factor that is relevant when we are thinking specifically about our movement is that during the period since Seattle, dissent has come to mean traveling long distances, staying in difficult circumstances, taking to the streets in militant actions that highlight civil disobedience and street fighting, and even risking arrest and severe mistreatment.

If we just pause a minute and think about it, it is obvious that this is a lot to ask of people at any time, much less as their first entry into activism. For example, how many of those now participating in events like the protests against the FTAA meeting in Quebec would have done so if they had to jump from total non-involvement to their current level of activity in one swoop, as their first political act? Consider people who are in their thirties or older, people who often have pressing family responsibilities, people who hold jobs and need to keep them for fear of disastrous consequences for themselves and the people they love. How many such folks are likely to join a demonstration that seems to demand as a prerequisite great mobility and to involve high risks as their initial step in becoming active?

The Trajectory of Change

The irony in all this is that the efficacy of civil disobedience and other militant tactics is not something that can be determined a priori. It resides, instead, in the connection between such militant practices and a growing movement of dissidents, many of whom are not in a position to support such protest tactics but who certainly support their logic and are moving in that direction. What gives civil disobedience and other militant manifestations the power to force elites to submit to our demands is not their own immediate militancy, but the fear that such events forebode a threatening firestorm of still more activism. However, if a sit-in or street battle of 2,000 or even 10,000 people has no larger, visible, supporting dissident community spread out across the land and from which the ranks of those sitting-in or battling will be replenished and even grow, this poses no serious threat to elites.

In other words, dissent that appears to have reached a plateau, regardless of how high that plateau may be, has no forward trajectory and is therefore manageable. Plateau-ed dissent is an annoyance that the state can control with clean-up crews or repression. In contrast, dissent that has a capacity to keep growing, even when much smaller, is more threatening and thus more powerful.

Civil disobedience involving a few thousand people, with ten or twenty times as many at associated massive rallies and marches, and with all these folks going back to organize local events that are in sum still larger, confronts elites with a very dangerous dynamic. In this scenario, not only are experienced activists continually refining and enlarging their commitment through personal encounters, print, audio, and video messaging, teach-ins, rallies, and marches, but new folks are moving from lack of knowledge to more knowledge and from rejecting demonstrations to supporting them and, when circumstances permit, to joining them. A huge and growing mass of dissident humanity can restrict government options for dealing with the most militant dissenters. This is what we seek — not a plateau of dissent (however honorable and courageous our efforts may be), but a trajectory of forward-moving growth that elites must worry about and will eventually succumb to.

If the state can create an image in which the only people who should come out to demonstrate are those who are already eager for or at least prepared to deal with gas, clubs, and "extended vacations," then we are not going to find parents with their young babies in strollers, elderly folks who couldn't take running through gas, young adults kept away from danger by parents concerned for their well-being, or average working people of all kinds unable to risk an unpredictable time away from work at our demonstrations.

Add to the difficulty of attending national rallies the insufficient means to manifest one's concerns and develop one's allegiances locally, and the movement is pushed toward a plateau condition. Then add that the movement's most learned and committed members are becoming slowly but steadily more focused not on communicating issues and goals to wider audiences, but on discussing street tactics and police methods that they are having to deal with (but which others have no useful comprehension of and are mostly just scared by), and the problem intensifies.

Add that under the pressure of preparing for and dealing with repression, activists get caught up in the notion that it is the battle that matters, and even get caught up in a kind of escalating choice of tactics, ignoring the fact that the police can always trump militancy, and the problem may become acute.

So even as we celebrate Seattle, Quebec, and Prague, I worry that we may be creating seeds for an enlarging operational disconnect between the movement and certain types of organizing, and therefore between the movement and the uninvolved but potentially receptive public.

I know this assessment — even moderated by recognition of all that has been accomplished and that there are people in fact now working on precisely these very problems — will sound harsh to many folks. But it is important to acknowledge that these matters need more attention.

Consider but one example. The Internet is a powerful tool, useful in many ways to our work. But with the Internet, we are communicating mostly with folks who want to hear what we have to say. They come to our sites and participate in our lists because they are already part of our movement. How else would they know where to find us?

This is similar to what occurs with a print periodical or a radio show that we might have in our arsenal of left institutions. The people who hear our message are those who subscribe or who listen knowing that they want to hear what we have to say. Don't get me wrong. This is very good. I have spent much of my life working on such efforts, which I feel are an important part of advancing our own awareness, insights, solidarity, and commitment, of refining our methods and agendas, and of tooling and retooling ourselves for the tasks at hand. The trouble is, if this is done without prioritizing other more face-to-face and public activity, it can lead to us (intentionally or not) becoming a kind of breakaway lead group dashing ahead and largely distancing ourselves from the constituencies who we most need to communicate with.

Another kind of organizing is explicit outreach, aimed not at solidifying and intensifying the knowledge and commitment of those who already speak our language and share our agendas, but at reaching people who differ with us. This is what we're doing when we hand out leaflets or do agit-prop and guerrilla theater in public places. This is what happens when we hold public rallies or teach-ins and we don't only e-mail those who are already eager to come to them, but, in addition and as our main priority, go door-to-door in our neighborhoods or on our campuses, urging, cajoling, inducing, and even pressuring folks to come to the events who would otherwise not do so.

Even more important, in many respects, this is what happens when we just go out of our way to engage new people in conversation, debate, and exploration. Face-to-face interaction with people who don't agree with us already, or who even disagree strongly with us, is at the heart of movement building. It is harder and scarier than communicating with those who share our views, of course, but it is even more important to do. We won't all prioritize it, but we can't all ignore it.

If we build our demonstrations in ways that make us all steadily less disposed and less able to do this kind of outreach, we are on a downhill track. Suppose, for example, that we are on a major campus like the football-focused one in State College, Pennsylvania, where I recently spoke. If our core movement of a couple of hundred folks spends almost all its time relating together and to people very like themselves, and almost none of its time going into sports bars and fraternities and all the other campus venues where 40,000 other students congregate, how are we going to become a majority project?

The Trajectory of Change

It takes great courage, commitment, and knowledge to become radical on such a campus, and to then work for and go to a demonstration miles away, whether in Quebec or Washington, D.C. But there is another step necessary in movement building, and it also takes courage: to become adept at going into that local sports bar and drumming up a conversation, over and over, with the folks who we need to win over to our movement.

To the extent outreach and consciousness raising is going to touch, entice, and retain new people in our movements, it has to offer them ways to maintain contact with activism and thereby sustain and build on their initial interest. If the end point of a face-to-face conversation about the IMF, for example, is that we urge someone to travel 500 or 1,000 or 5,000 miles to a demonstration, to sleep on a floor or not sleep at all, and to take to the streets in conflict in a setting where we and the media lead them to expect to be gassed and to face arrest and extended detention that might keep them away from school, much less kids and jobs, few if any newcomers are going to jump in. But, if they don't do that, and they have nothing obvious and meaningful to do short of that, then there is no way that these newly aroused people can retain contact with the committed activist community that has piqued their dissident interest. As a result, their anger will most likely dissipate in the fog imposed by daily life and mainstream media.

Without mechanisms that not only reach out, but also preserve and enforce the initial impact of our outreach, new folks won't take hold in our movement. We will plan the next demonstration. We will go to it. We will celebrate. But it will be with mostly the same crowd as at the last one. Yes, the activists won widespread support from the surrounding community in Quebec, which is a fantastic accomplishment. But then what? And what about 50 miles from our sites of conflict, or 1,000 miles, and then some?

The point to keep foremost in our minds is that we are not fighting a little battle that a small army of dissidents can win. Globalization matters a lot to the money mongers. They will not give in easily. They will alter their methods, change their venues, hide their efforts, and rhetorically sugarcoat their plans, seemingly tirelessly. And whenever activists rush out too far from their base of support, those elites will pounce, with vigor.

The Trajectory of Change

For us to win, and that's what matters, we must attain massive proportions. We must always have the growth of our movement forefront in our minds. I think the experience of masses of people having their interest roused but then having no way to become comfortably involved threatens to prevent our efforts from being overwhelmingly powerful and victorious.

We don't need to eliminate our more militant tactics. Not at all. But we do need to give them greater meaning and strength by incorporating with them much more outreach; organizing many more events and activities that have more diverse and introductory levels of participation; creating more local means for ongoing involvement by people just getting interested; and especially by spending more time clarifying issues, aims, and the logic of our activity to new audiences who don't yet agree with our efforts.

Our current trajectory of change didn't start in Seattle. It didn't end in Quebec. And it most immediately needs to get much bigger, rather than still more militant.

NEW TARGETS

We anti-globalists oppose imperial trade arrangements. We repudiate a world in which the rich get richer and the poor get poorer. We laugh at pundits claiming that globalization positively entwines world centers via new modes of communication and travel. We laugh at the claim that globalization expands democracy and participation. We live and breathe that globalization is another name for re-writing international norms of commerce, power, and culture to benefit the already rich and powerful still more. We see that it further elevates U.S. and European elites. We feel that it weakens national governments and populations. We know that it strengthens elite conclaves of corporate bosses. In short, for us, globalization is twenty-first-century imperialism. It has to be stopped.

But given that we are against international inequity and injustice, mustn't we also oppose domestic inequity and injustice? As central institutions of international impoverishment, the WTO, IMF, and World Bank provide obvious targets. What about the White House? What about Wall Street? What about local Chambers of Commerce? What about major corporations themselves? What about the information managers that trumpet globalization, from NBC and CBS to local talk radio, and from the *New York Times* and *Washington Post* to local tabloids? And what about the presidential palaces, stock exchanges, corporations, and mainstream media from Britain to Thailand, Peru to Australia, Canada to Japan, and Brazil to India?

If we are against profit-seeking, authoritarian usurping of power, and media manipulation of information, mustn't we be for just allocations of resources and wealth, decision making that gives each actor a say over their lives and circumstances, and cultures that respect truth and address the needs of large populations? Against profit and competition, we advocate equity and cooperation. Against exclusion and authority, we advocate participation and self-management. Against lies and manipulation, we advocate truth and honest exchange.

Our anti-globalization activism is an international phenomenon, a very serious business. At stake are not only critical institutions like the IMF and World Bank, but also the capitalist market and ownership relations that engender "globalization" in the first place.

To attain the size, comprehension, and commitment to not only stir up people's awareness — but to galvanize this into sustained activism and to then parlay that sustained activism into actions that increase the social costs to the point where elites can no longer pursue their destructive aims — we need to design movement agendas that inspire widespread interest and provide means for widespread ongoing participation. We need movement focuses that are diverse and multiple, that are local, national, and international, and that are continuous, not just annual or bi-annual events.

So which way forward for anti-globalization?

The anti-globalization movement needs to highlight what it is aiming for. We need to clarify our alternatives for international relations and also what we mean by a cooperative and just economy able to improve people's lives domestically, as well as internationally. We need to crystallize our rejection of authoritarian trade institutions, but also to explain our attitude toward corporations and markets, and our vision of what could replace them.

Michael Albert

Attaining shared goals won't happen by magic hand-waving. We won't conquer the vision problem unless we address such matters together, debate them, explore them, begin to attain some useful agreements about them, and then put the results forth as widely as we can. The media and, more importantly, our potential political allies repeatedly ask us, "What do you want?" Making headway requires that we answer intelligently, convincingly, and passionately.

We need to re-emphasize reaching out as widely as possible and providing means of participation for as many new people as we can interest in our efforts. We need to unequivocally understand that our strategic goal isn't to have a small army of courageous, creative, insightful, and bold dissidents. We need many in motion, not few, no matter how good the few may be. For our goals, thousands and even tens of thousands are still too few.

We have to correct the appearance that opposing capitalist globalization requires traveling to distant cities and demonstrating in the midst of clubs and tear gas, much less hurling paving stones and dodging rubber bullets. Few people will jump from no involvement to such confrontation in one vast leap, even if they may become highly militant at some point in the future. And few people are in position to do this. They don't have the time, the freedom, or the funds. They aren't physically, emotionally, familially, or occupationally in a position to join us, or they doubt the efficacy of our tactics.

So, the facts are simple:

(i) A movement that can win change in international trade relations needs millions and even tens of millions, not merely thousands, of participants.

(ii) People aren't really movement participants unless they are doing things in a sustained and ongoing way within the movement.

(iii) To grow sufficiently enough that we can win, our movement needs to offer things for people to do where they live and in accord with their dispositions and possibilities.

The Indy Media Centers (IMCs) are an amazing and glorious outgrowth of the anti-globalization project. But what if these new organizations located all around the world were to take up a second agenda? The IMCs are now committed and should remain committed to finding new ways to convey dissenting information to local audiences. But what about also becoming the nuclei around which activism against mainstream media can gel?

What about Indy Media organizations sponsoring regional gatherings that set up organizing projects to raise consciousness about mainstream media and to then plan and carry out mass rallies and other demonstrations directed at mainstream media? Wouldn't that add a new dimension, a new set of focuses, and a whole new tone and dynamic to our movement?

To win, we need to generate a trajectory of activism that elites cannot easily repress or manipulatively derail, and which they also can't calmly abide. That is the logic of social change in the near and even middle term.

But what threatens elites that cannot be readily repressed away or derailed? The only answer I know of is rapidly growing numbers of dissidents, varied diversifying focuses of their dissent, and steadily escalating commitment and militancy of their tactics.

To succeed, then:

New Targets

(i) Our movements need to involve multiple tactics in ways that help each constituency manifest its aims without the efforts of a few trumping all visibility, tone, and content of the rest.

(ii) Our movements need to involve multiple issues, enabling each constituency to mount its priority claims and aspirations, with none drowning out the others and each finding means to support the rest. (For example, globalization activists could mobilize on behalf of the work of living-wage activists, of unionists striking their employers, of anti-war activists opposing Plan Colombia, and with people of color organizing against police repression, racist violence, and impoverishment.)

(iii) Our movements need to have a militant edge that creatively displays a rising tide of anger and commitment, but which also remains in close touch with the main body of the movement, operating to propel its growth.

If aggressive civil disobedience is the largest manifestation of our opposition to the targets we pick, we will have little power. But if aggressive civil disobedience grows naturally from a growing mass of broader dissent — with hundreds of thousands and then millions of people in country after country involved no less visibly than those who are most confrontational — then we will be on the road to serious social change.

Finally, we also need some clarity about violence. It's really quite simple. The state has a monopoly of violence. What that means is that there is no way for the public, particularly in developed first world societies, to compete on the field of violence with their governments. That ought to be obvious.

Our strong suit is information, facts, justice, disobedience, and especially numbers. In sum: politics. Their strong suit is lying and especially exerting military power. A contest of escalating violence is a contest we are doomed to lose. A contest in which numbers, commitment, and increasingly militant nonviolent activism confronts state power is a contest we can win.

Yes, the impetus to manifest anger is powerful. But there is nothing courageous or strategic about charting a path directly into the lion's mouth. Our tactical sense must be combined with strategic plans carefully aimed at winning. We can have teach-ins. We can have rallies. We can have marches. We can have strikes. We can build our own blockades. We can utilize all manner of creativity and playfulness in our dissent. We can go out and talk to people. We can obstruct. We can destroy property when doing so sends a clear and coherent message. We can hurl back tear gas canisters in self defense, and tear down walls and other obstacles to remain mobile.

But to attack the police with the intent of doing bodily harm, whether with stones or Molotov cocktails, simply invites further escalation of their violence. It does nothing to hinder elite agendas. Instead, it propels and legitimates them. Anger-fed violence is hard to avoid in some situations. But avoid it we must.

BEING RADICAL

Suppose you find capitalist globalization (or any other systemic oppression) horrific. You reject rewriting the rules of international exchange to further enrich the already rich and empower the already powerful. But how can you direct your personal energies to impact such an immense process as globalization (or racism, or sexism, or exploitation, or authoritarianism)? How can individuals transcend futile whining? How can we improve lives now? How can we bring nearer a truly liberated social commonwealth in our future?

When we pursue radical politics, most of us come to a point when we try to examine society and its dynamics, understand something about the agents of change, and figure out how we can act upon the world to make it better.

So, to start, we have to get a feeling about society. Such feelings rely on facts such as that more than 30 million people live below the poverty level in the United States. If you made $200,000 a day, five days a week, it would take you more than 300 years to earn as much as Bill Gates is worth, even if his wealth didn't grow in the meantime.

Michael Albert

At a lower but still barely imaginable level, when Michael Jordan was last playing professional basketball with the Chicago Bulls (before he became an owner of the Washington Wizards), he made $300,000 per game and, with endorsements, roughly $150,000 per day. Assuming Jordan slept seven hours a night, he was making about $52,000 while he slept. While he attended an average movie, he made $12,550. While eating a meal, he made about $5,000. Yet, even Michael Jordan would have had to save everything he made from his income at that high rate for more than 100 years to attain the current net worth of Bill Gates. That gives some grasp of income distribution in the United States, as long as we remember the huge masses of people for whom a minuscule fraction of this income would be grounds for virtually unlimited celebration.

Other relevant facts include that U.S. society fosters approximately 250 reported rapes daily, with perhaps 10 times that number going unreported. Black infant mortality in the United States is twice that of whites, with Latinos not far off that mark. U.S. society engenders one successful suicide every 20 minutes, with one attempt every other minute. In the United States, capitalist firms spend $125 billion every year to advertise to people who have what's called "discretionary income" — which is roughly 17 percent of the population — while the rest of the population is disposable.

The United States has 3 million people without homes to sleep in, though it has roughly 50,000 hotels that are generally only about half full and are able to house 15 million people. So, the United States has 3 million homeless people with 7.5 million empty rooms that they could, but can't, occupy.

The United States includes working people who profoundly hate the doctors, lawyers, engineers, and managers who lord over them with their high incomes and status and dismissive superiority and arrogance, yet devote their lives to making it possible for their children to become one of these despised agents of authority. The United States has town after town where in terms of the number of participants the main social and convivial gathering place is either a bar or an Alcoholics Anonymous meeting.

This picture of the United States extends abroad, as well, to Bolivia, with its tin miners who have a life expectancy of 35 years due to the practices of U.S. companies like Alcoa; to India, where 10,000 children a year are going blind for want of a vitamin that could be provided by the United States at the cost of a nickel per child, but isn't; and to the Dominican Republic, where workers earn 25 to 50 cents an hour so that U.S. multinationals can properly profit, and then are repressed or disappeared by local police forces trained by the U.S. military to defend the system of advantage against those who even try to disobey. Around the globe, on the order of 50,000 children die every day of starvation and preventable diseases.

Awareness of this kind of horror leads many people to oppose injustice and criminality, and to seek a world that embodies a more humane logic, with more life-affirming institutions. And when people become moved by that kind of insight, opposition, and aspiration, they begin to try to understand society.

Most often nowadays, we begin to conceive of society as a conglomeration of entwined institutions that interactively create the opportunities or the constraints that largely govern our lives. And the institutions we begin to highlight are of particular types: economic institutions like corporations and markets; kinship institutions like the nuclear family; cultural institutions like nations, religions, and racial communities; and political institutions like legislatures, courts, and the police.

Moving deeper into this oppositional mindset, becoming steadily more aroused against institutional injustices, activists begin to see these structures that impose limits on people's lives as being entwined with one another. The institutions become for us, in sum, the preposterously insane thing that we intuitively call "the system."

We see how the influences from the system's component institutions emanate, mold, and shape each other, so the economy pushes our families, and the way we socialize and interact sexually in our living units in turn impacts the economy. Likewise, how we deliberate and make decisions in the polity affects our cultures, and our cultures in turn impact our courts and legislatures. And so on, around and around. Economic relations, race relations, gender relations, and political relations each impact the nature and structure of the rest. Each reproduce the defining logic of the others.

And we see, as well, that these various institutions and derivative structures that mediate our life options also divide us into groups that we need to highlight in our thinking: classes, gender groups, cultural communities, racial communities, political parties, and the like. As we move into this mindset of opposition, we see that these different groups — men and women, gays and straights, Latinos, blacks, Catholics, Jews, politicians, workers, professionals (or "coordinators," as I prefer to call them), and capitalists — generally develop different material interests and associated behaviors and consciousnesses based on the effects of the institutions by which they are defined. They struggle and contest with each other, with some of these groups located at the bottom of hierarchies in our society, while others enjoy great privilege and power in its uppermost positions.

Reaching this point, our unfolding social comprehension is moving clearly leftward and may gather sufficient momentum and confidence to lead us to try and understand not only more about these defining institutions and their effects on us, but also about alternative institutions. We then explore a possible vision we can aspire to, a vision of a world no longer dominated by corporations, markets, and hierarchically defined cultures, families, and states and without the suffering they impose on us.

When we move to find alternatives, we may begin to ask ourselves: how do we accomplish the needed tasks and positive functions that the corporations, markets, states, courts, churches, schools, families, and other institutions in society now achieve, but in ways that serve people positively and foster human fulfillment and development? How do we get rid of the bathwater of oppressive institutions and not only keep, but also nurture and fully actualize, the baby of needed social functions?

When we start to move in this direction, we have to try and decide in more substantial detail *what we're for.* Here we don't all agree, as yet, but one view is that we favor equity, solidarity, diversity, and self-management. The resources, services, and products of human labors should be distributed in a manner that is fair and accords with moral aspirations, as well as getting economic tasks done. The products of our labors should be distributed to people in accordance with the effort and sacrifice they put into their creation.

Michael Albert

People's circumstances should be comparably pleasant or onerous, rather than some people enjoying superior circumstances and some people suffering from oppressive circumstances. People's circumstances should equally empower. We should live in a society based on solidarity, in which for us to do better, others have to do better too, instead of living in a society in which for me to do better somebody else has to do worse. We should have a society in which diversity is not only respected but welcomed and celebrated because we can all benefit and have richer lives as a result.

We should live in a society in which people have control over the decisions that determine the character of their lives and have that control in proportion to how they are affected by those decisions, manifesting their preferences through appropriate democratic structures.

If we have views more or less like the ones I have just described, the question arises: what kinds of institutions would fulfill those values? Here I think leftists have been lax, or worse. Thirty years ago, we developed movements at a time when people in the United States really felt that the suffering and pain people endured were personal problems.

Being Radical

Poverty was a personal failing. Being battered was a personal failing. Even being raped was a personal failing. Suffering the indignities of racism was a personal failing. All these issues were personal. They didn't have a collective dimension for many people. Then movements came along and identified the collective effects, and particularly the collective causes — the social, structural, and institutional causes — of these problems. Michael Harrington wrote a book about poverty called *The Other America,* making the case that poverty existed and that it wasn't just a question of personal inadequacies but was widespread and socially caused.[1] That was a very powerful claim, and it had a tremendous impact on many people who didn't really see poverty that way until they read *The Other America* and met activists teaching that lesson who awoke in them certain hidden truths.

Likewise, the women's movement came along and said that the abuses women suffer — battering, rape, and all manner of indignities and denials of their capacity to fulfill themselves — weren't a function of the inadequacies of individual women, but were systematic social problems. When women talked to each other about these revelations, they saw that their life experiences were very similar, not because they all accidentally had the same personal failing, but because their problems were a function of the whole social structure imposing pain on them. When women saw this, it opened their eyes. They became very angry at the injustice of it, and movements arose.

This change in consciousness happened not only about poverty and sexism, but about racism, through a civil rights movement that really initiated and was the spine and heart of the new activism; about war and peace; about the environment; and later about sexuality, as well.

These were immensely important developments, but the trouble is that for the last 30 years we have been trying to build movements the same way as we did at the outset, even though everybody already long since knows that the pains of social life are largely systemic. We keep talking about how bad everything is, and how problems we identify are systemic, but it is no longer eye-opening to say that the system causes these ills, and it hasn't been for a long time.

When the left goes out and communicates to people that society causes these pains and these ills nowadays, we're really telling people something that at a deep level they already know. We're telling people something that nobody among those who are suffering is truly contesting anymore. Yet there is something that people don't know, which is whether or not anything better is possible for them and their loved ones, whether or not they or anyone can attain anything better. Addressing that question is the pressing task, a task to which we haven't been giving enough attention.

In today's environment, considerably less time should be spent on explaining to people just how big and powerful the system is, and enumerating all the manifold ways it hurts us. Most often, enumerating the ills is not inspiring, or anger-provoking, but is instead just depressing, debilitating, and deadening. This is not to say that we should avoid clarifying how institutions work, but to do only that doesn't inspire activity. The real obstacle to movement building in the United States is not a widespread notion that everything is fine but the idea that despite how bad things are, nothing better is possible.

We need to convey some understanding of a better system, some understanding of how to reach it — indeed, enough of both to provide hope, grounding, and positive orientation for ourselves and those who are joining our movements.

As folks become radical — as they see the systemic roots of limitations on people's lives, and vow to uproot those roots — what is a broad vision for change in the United States? What is a strategy for reaching it?

Strategy is an accumulation of tactics. We meld tactics together into something that we might call campaigns. These campaigns meld together into something that we might call a scenario of change. These scenarios involve people who are the agents of change engaging in the struggle. They also involve structures that we use to express our powers and organize our energies. So, a strategy is going to be some conception that combines an understanding of:

(i) who it is that's going to make change

(ii) in what kinds of numbers

(iii) in what kinds of structures and organizational forms will they organize themselves

(iv) what kinds of issues they will address

(v) which tactics they're going to use when fighting for change

(vi) how they're going to combine all those tactics into campaign gains, and

(vii) how these campaigns are going to not only better people's lives now, but also lead in time to new institutions.

That's what strategy is all about. We don't win all at once but in a sequence of steps. We continually win new gains along a road that leads to fundamental changes.

How do we win new gains along the road? We raise the social cost of not granting the gains we seek until we reach the point where those who don't want to give in to our demands have no choice but to do so. Change is a combination of a sequence of reforms or limited victories that string together into a pattern in which we continually change the contours of the world that we live in, making ourselves stronger and making those who oppose change weaker until, ultimately, we win basic alterations.

What might a winning strategy look like? Think back to the 1960s, when we had various, powerful movements that, at the time, were doing some of what I have described. The women's movement at one point not only critiqued sexism but looked toward replacing specific institutions. It questioned traditional marriage. It questioned the isolated nuclear family. It tried to come up with alternatives emphasizing collective arrangements and parenting rather than sex-role-defined mothering and fathering.

In the 1960s, anti-racist movements questioned the basic composition of our culture, the ways in which communities form and relate to one another, and proposed alternatives based on mutual respect (or what was, at the time, called intercommunalism).

Anarchists and youth movement activists tried to figure out just exactly what a polity needed to do and how it could be done without engendering authoritarianism, while encouraging autonomy, collective responsibility, and participation.

Various movements in the 1960s not only critiqued existing reality but attempted to develop a positive program for what kind of society they wanted in the future.

Later — actually only a blink of an eye later in history, but quite a while in the lives of the many people involved — the Rainbow Coalition formed. Suppose the Rainbow Coalition had been a little clearer in its conception and seen itself as the greatest common sum of all those independent movements, those autonomous movements, already in existence. Autonomous movements existed then and will exist as well in the future because people propelled by the situations that they find themselves in will create movements organized around specific areas of society. We will continue to see labor, women's, ecology, anti-racist, gay, peace, and other movements. But none of them can win alone. That was the Rainbow message.

Suppose the concept of the Rainbow Coalition had been very clear about the coalition's need to be the greatest common sum of all its parts, rather than their least common denominator. Not a coalition in which you take whatever everybody can agree on, and you focus on that limited agenda, but a new type of encompassing structure in which you take the entire agenda of each component part, even where they don't agree. The encompassing agenda of the project would include all the various component parts, each of which may have disagreements with other aspects of the whole agenda. In this new type of conflicted but encompassing and solidaristic whole, we all find ourselves in a bigger structure. It has an agenda that we don't all entirely agree with, but which we stick with despite differences because we all respect each of its component movements and their insights, and thus what each component adds to the agenda.

Suppose we did that for our overarching movement, and we had the autonomous movements within it, as well, and a process by which we try to learn, to refine and develop the overall agenda, and have it inform all the component movements. Suppose we were also forming institutions in our communities, grass roots organizations of the people who live in communities, to begin to conceive of what it would be like to take some control over their own lives where they live. And suppose we were doing the same thing in workplaces, as well, forming councils of workers who are beginning to conceive of what it would be like to control their own situation and workplaces. In both of those cases, communities and workplaces, suppose these new structures fight for improvements and changes both to make life better now and also to increase their organizational strength and support for building toward still more improvements in the future.

Being Radical

Suppose all of these aspects of activism were developing simultaneously, and we were fighting to win new types of affirmative action, or fighting to win increased wages but not increases in the price of products, or fighting to curtail dumping, or to win full employment, or to curb globalization or military interventions, or to win new access to local and national decision-making influence, or to win gains around other gender, race, political, economic, or ecological issues. And suppose, over time, this whole structure begins to educate and to incorporate wider and wider sectors of people.

How could we build a movement such as this? First, there are some obvious ways that a movement clearly doesn't grow. It doesn't grow if it creates a culture that is hostile to the people who it's trying to organize. We're not going to have that whole aroused left get larger and larger and larger until it involves 35 or 40 percent of the population, with the rest mostly just standing by the side and a few opposing it, if we are antagonizing most citizens.

These are the rough conditions we need to win really transcendent changes. And we're not going to be able to do that if the movement we build has a culture hostile to working people — if, for example, we have a culture that reflects the attributes of a law school instead of a working-class bar, so to speak. Such a movement is not going to welcome into active membership 40 percent of the population. Being class elitist will hinder growth among working people in the same way that having a movement whose culture, dynamics, structure, and behavior are grossly sexist or racist will hinder growth among women, blacks, and Latinos.

Our movement doesn't have to be antagonistic to critical constituencies to fail. All it has to be is uncongenial enough that it will be uncomfortable and disempowering for centrally important sectors of the population, be it the working class, women, racial groups, or religious groups.

You can't possibly begin to reach a truly large sector of people in the United States if your movements are unwelcoming to these constituencies. So it follows that the kind of movement we need to develop is one that's inclusive, which means that it has to respect and grow out of the attitudes, beliefs, and behavior patterns of real people in society — not out of some abstract perfect people, or worse, out of a tiny narrow sector of people with unusual advantages.

Being Radical

Yet, at the same time, this broad project also has to move toward creating the new kinds of values and modes of interrelating that we desire.

Notes

1   Michael Harrington, *The Other America: Poverty in the United States* (New York: Scribner, 1997). The original Penguin edition was published in 1962.

BEING CONGENIAL

OR, THE STICKINESS PROBLEM

Some time back I spoke at a National Green gathering about "movement building." My initial idea was to discuss the progressive and left community's outreach problem. We try to reach potential allies in society and to "reel them in" to full participation. Not enough people hear us. Our outreach problem involves our organizing methods, campaigns, and demands and how they appeal to people, but also our need for "a megaphone" loud enough to reach beyond audiences already seeking us out. We need our own progressive mass media.

But as I thought about movement building, I realized there was another problem that was even worse than outreach because it was more debilitating and we had less of an excuse for it.

Think of the progressive/left community as a team fighting against both apathy and also outright support for the status quo. Call it Team Change. Size isn't the only variable affecting Team Change's strength, for sure, but without numbers we aren't going far, so we must reach out more widely. But as we do reach out and win people's attention or involvement, do we then keep them committed? Let's call this the "stickiness problem."

To win fundamental change, and that is our purpose, Team Change needs a force field that draws potential team members steadily leftward ever more strongly the closer it attracts them. First a person hears about some facet of Team Change. There is an attraction, however slight. As the person is drawn closer, the attraction must increase to offset counter-pressures from society to avoid Team Change. Once a person joins Team Change, the attraction should sustain permanent membership.

Do we have this kind of community seeking radical change in society? To decide, we can look at

(i) the historical experience that Team Change has had with potential recruits in the past and

(ii) the characteristics of Team Change

to see whether its attractive force escalates as people get closer to steady involvement.

Consider the past 30 years of activism. How many people have heard about, come into contact with, worked with, or become part of Team

Being Congenial

Change who no longer have anything much to do with it? The number, I think, is in the millions — perhaps 10 million or more.

This includes folks from the civil rights movement, the movement against the Vietnam War, and the women's movement. It includes those who have been No Nukers. It includes everyone who has worked in truly progressive local projects, Green movements, student movements, and various left electoral campaigns.

This includes anyone who has taken a course from a radical teacher, read a left book, gone to talks or demonstrations, listened to progressive radio, or read left periodicals. Anyone who was part of the anti–Gulf War movement, the anti-apartheid movement, or the various Latin American solidarity movements counts in this total. So do those who have been in gay and lesbian movements, pro-choice campaigns, community and consumer movements, union organizing campaigns, labor struggles, anti-racist campaigns, strikes, and boycotts. Ten million is a conservative estimate.

Of these millions of people, how many are still an active part of Team Change? When I faced up to this gap between those we at some time or other reached, however tentatively, and those who are now actively involved, I was shocked.

If you think in terms of a year or two, the left's outreach problem, not our ability to hold onto people once we attract them, seems paramount. The usual way this concern is expressed is to ask: how do we get beyond the choir? But if you think about a decade or two, then the left's stickiness problem demands attention. The gap between possibility and actuality is at the heart of our prospects for social change.

Let's come at it from another angle. Why should someone, once at least somewhat attracted to the logic, dynamics, and programs of the progressive community, become more attracted and stick to it? Conversely, why do people feel steadily less attachment as time passes, only to return to the mainstream?

Think of a person getting more and more involved with progressive ideas and activity. Does this person merge into a growing community of people, feel more secure and appreciated, feel a growing sense of personal worth and of contribution to something valuable, and enjoy a sense of accomplishment? Are this person's needs better met than before, while he or she is making a contribution to improving others lives, as well?

Or does this person meet a lot of other people who continually question her motives and behaviors, making her feel insecure and constantly criticized? Does this person feel diminishing personal worth and doubt that what he or she is doing is making a difference for anyone? Does he suspect there is little accomplished, and no daily, weekly, or monthly evidence of progress?

Does she have needs that were previously met but that are now unmet, and few new ones addressed? Is this person's life getting more frustrating, less enjoyable? Does it seem she is only bothering other people, and rarely doing anything meaningful on their behalf?

Does she find herself ever less aware of what "the left" is or stands for, or even repulsed by its vague or bitter attributes, rather than attracted to its clarity, insights, and successes?

You might ask different questions than I have, but I think the point is clear enough.

Let's stretch the Team Change analogy. Imagine a football, baseball, basketball, or soccer team. Whether it is high school, college, or professional doesn't matter. Suppose it doesn't improve its results as time passes. At some point, the coach looks at the choices that have been made, the strategies that have been used, the norms that have been employed and says, "Hold on, we have to make some corrections."

Since our Team Change has no coach and it needs to be participatory and democratic, being self-critical is everyone's responsibility, not that of some maximum leader. But Team Change must also play to win if it is concerned with more than mere posturing. And that means we need to reassess how we organize ourselves, the culture of our movements, what we learn as we become more committed, how we interrelate, and what benefits and responsibilities we have due to our political involvement.

The alternative to doing much better regarding movement stickiness is another long losing season, perhaps two or three decades worth. Unlike the case of an inflexible high school, college, or professional ball club, this means hundreds of millions of lives unnecessarily ended for want of our greater success and final victory.

Being Congenial

Being right about what's wrong with society and why it is wrong, and even being able to convey all this to wide audiences, isn't enough. Movements must be clear about goals and strategy to retain a sense of purpose, confidence, identity, and integrity in the face of critique.

They have to be structured and function in ways that not only enlarge but retain membership, and that not only contribute to change but do so clearly in all their members' eyes. They have to not only attack problems, but to meet needs for members and populations more broadly, and they have to win victories that meet needs but also create the conditions for still more victories to follow.

The absence of all this is at the root of our stickiness problem.

Some reasons for this have to do with our lack of a compelling guiding vision and strategy, our unclear class allegiances, and our continuing inability to combine respect for desirable autonomies and for essential solidarities in a single encompassing movement.

Others will have different notions. But we need to at least agree that it is a priority for the left that we enumerate the possibilities, assess them, and then develop clear plans for overcoming our stickiness problem. If we don't manage this much, I fear we will be running in ever narrowing circles, with a movement of diehards rather than astute social critics, when we need to be reaching ever widening numbers of people to effect change.

RESPECTING DIFFERENCES

WHILE BUILDING SOLIDARITY

Collective social struggle bringing together large numbers of people into acts of dissent will never be perfectly choreographed, but we can at least have broad guidelines that would benefit all involved constituencies.

One desirable norm is that people influence decisions in proportion to the extent that the events being decided affect them. A minority should not impose itself by trumping other's choices. A majority should not dictate all the ways one can protest.

A second desirable norm is diversity. Movements should welcome many different approaches as people's right, but also recognize that what one doesn't agree with at the moment could in the long run prove superior. Moreover, an exciting mix of movement approaches almost always improves on boring homogeneity.

Solidarity is a third desirable norm. Movement members should not only be civil to one another, but also care about every participant's well being, conditions, views, and mutual interrelations.

So how do we democratically conduct large-scale movements that include diverse and disagreeing constituencies of different sizes and viewpoints? Suppose that the progressive communities decide to call major demonstrations around the biotechnology industry, the IMF, or the World Bank. Suppose the anti-WTO movement, the anti-corporate movements, Greens, prison movements, consumer movements, disability rights movements, anti-sweatshop movements, anti-racist movements, the women's movement, and the queer movement are all planning to be involved. How can we go to Washington, New York, or Los Angeles, or wherever else makes sense, or operate with large numbers more locally, and come out the other side or our events stronger and more unified?

One scenario says groups with the most money and outreach should decide tactics to be employed, who's welcome, and even what slogans are permitted. But obviously this won't bring about democracy, diversity, and solidarity.

Respecting Differences

A second scenario says we create a broad umbrella coalition around a laundry list of mutually agreed upon demands and actions that all participants accept. But what if other important and differing coalitions and constituencies come to town?

A third "self-managing" scenario favors protests becoming the sum total of their many components, rather than embodying a single organization's priorities or the agenda of a single leading coalition. With this approach, the organizations, coalitions, and constituencies coming to town for a massive display of dissent mutually negotiate the final schedule, which ends up being an amalgamation of everyone's agendas.

With the third approach you get a rally that highlights a speaker that some constituencies don't like; a street intersection that is blocked by civil disobedience that some constituencies don't favor; a building that is the focus of more militant tactics advocated by only a small minority. But everyone understands that they all need to make room for and even welcome one another in ways that maximize mutual impact, respect individual differences, and diminish conflicts and internal disputes. The third perspective encourages different organizations and coalitions working on massive future protests not only to bring people and their own events to town, but also to incorporate as much diversity in shared venues as possible and, when that isn't possible, to incorporate controversial activities in separate venues, without curtailing each other's agendas. The marchers march, the civil disobedience people carry out civil disobedience, the direct action advocates do direct actions. Different participating organizations and coalitions bring their own demands, speakers, and methods.

The process of talking through the tactics and focuses that different constituencies, organizations, and coalitions bring to the project hopefully brings mutual cooperation. When efforts can occur in a shared space, that's excellent. But when constituencies need their own separate space and time so they do not crowd out one another, that's fine too. Decisions come about via open discussion of the involved organizing groups, coalitions, networks, and constituencies. On top of whatever other approaches participants bring to major movement projects, wouldn't it therefore be desirable to have an overarching commitment to negotiations, planning, and seeking as much solidarity and mutual respect as can be attained?

This model still leaves the problem of ruling out unacceptable tactics or views, police provocation, and the like. But open negotiation is the best option for isolating out-of-touch elements so as to make their exclusion obvious to all, even while incorporating the widest array, most exciting assemblage, and most powerful combination of forces possible.

Participatory democracy isn't easy, particularly when we are operating in an authoritarian and regimented society. But even with all its dangers and difficulties, real participatory democracy is by far the best chance we have to effectively utilize our talents, commitments, and energies on behalf of winning valuable immediate gains while building movements that can go even further.

AUTONOMY WITHIN SOLIDARITY

One of the pervasive problems of the U.S. left is fragmentation. One of the abiding strengths of the U.S. left is diversity. How do we overcome the former without losing the latter?

People do not automatically develop multi-focused political priorities. We have different life experiences which sensitize us to some aspects of social life more than others. We suffer some pains more than others, discern some oppressions more aggressively than others, pursue some agendas more militantly than others. When we dissent, we often focus on one oppression more than on others and on one intellectual and activist "orientation" more than on others. We develop movements of national, racial, and cultural communities; of women, gays and lesbians, workers, and young people; and around such focuses as race, religious bigotry, gender, sexuality, poverty and class, authority, war and peace, and ecology.

The downside of this multi-facetedness is that none of these agendas can be accomplished by only those who see it as their first priority. A single vast apparatus with many mutually enforcing dimensions enforces these oppressions. It is too damn powerful and too damn entrenched, both in institutions and in people's behaviors, to succumb to partial assaults. Separate efforts dilute our strength and compete for allegiance, priority, resources, and status.

The upside of this multi-facetedness is that each separate effort better utilizes the insights of those most attuned to the complexities of its focus than would any single orientation subsuming all the rest. Trying to use one single orientation inevitably subsumes much of what is dynamic and influential in each area, picking out only a few central features to address.

Worse, it might imperially extend the views characterizing one area — as when Marxism (or radical feminism or anarchism) elevates economics (or gender or the state) and "reduces" other phenomena in the process. This not only excludes important issues from our analysis; it often prescribes aims for the most oppressed, rather than fulfilling the needs they themselves determine to be the most important.

Autonomy Within Solidarity

So we criticize fragmenting into single-focused efforts because they weaken the total movement and even each component by fragmenting energies, inducing competitions, and so on. But we also appreciate these laser-focused efforts because they elevate the true needs of those who feel each type of oppression most directly. Think of the civil rights movement, the women's movement, the hippie movement, the labor movement, and the movement against the Vietnam War.

Or think of the more recent incarnations of these struggles, with the addition of the gay and lesbian movements, the Green movement, and even sub-movements among the unemployed, religious and racial sectors, or vegetarians and vegans. The strengths of focus and weaknesses of fragmentation are evident.

Now, we have still another round of focus and fragmentation: the New Party, the Labor Party, the Green Party, the Campaign for a New Tomorrow, the possibility that the National Organization for Women (NOW) might launch a party, plus multitudinous media projects, and an endless stream of single-issue national, regional, and local organizing efforts. Why isn't their more unity? Why don't lots of political parties, media projects, or organizing projects merge into a single encompassing party, media, or activist project?

Or, even better, why don't they merge with one another across these lines, into one big movement? Surely the gains in enlarged outreach, increased membership and power, and economies of scale are obvious. If each party, periodical, project, and movement is a potential thread in a large mosaic, why don't the threads intertwine so that we get a garment rather than just a jumble of discordant strings going nowhere?

Well, each party, project, periodical, and movement has little time for what they see as spurious efforts at unity that won't advance their day-to-day survival and may even siphon energies from it. More, each worries that in unity its priorities will be given only lip service, or worse. Each fears its voice, leaders, and vision will be subsumed by the scope of the larger ally or overrun by the energy of the smaller one.

Those groups that are larger bemoan the hassle of taking on other efforts involving peculiar people and their fanatical attention to peripheral or distracting issues. And those groups that are smaller wonder why they should dilute their serious intentions and risk subordination to the less radical views of larger efforts.

Regardless of size, everyone wonders: why should we reduce our prioritization of race, class, gender, sex, war, or ecology, or our special understanding and commitment and radicalism, by aligning with groups that have agendas emphasizing something we feel to be of lower priority, or insufficiently radical, or too extreme?

In the face of all these concerns, which have confronted movements for every day of every year of my politically involved life from roughly 1966 to now, I would like to offer a proposal for a way forward. It involves advocating a new kind of unity, advocating a new type of organizational structure and relations, and taking a few simple first steps.

In the past, "working together" has generally meant coalition. You take the agendas and understandings of each potential ally and survey them for features in common. Then a generally temporary coalition is built around the common aims. The process involves little mutual involvement. Each side tries to benefit itself in the context of a temporary intersection of some priorities. Of course, each ally tries to entice members from the other and to build its own constituency. If there is a way to subsume the ally, or infiltrate the ally, so that one's own organization is all that remains when the dust clears, that's fine.

Here is a different attitude. Suppose working together means merging agendas in a lasting larger framework designed to pursue collective efforts and mutual support, while also retaining them intact for one's own separate efforts. Using an example from the past, suppose the anti–Vietnam War movement, the hippies, the civil rights movement, the women's movement, and the national welfare rights movement from a few decades back were going to get together. It would always be for some limited event or project chosen because it was amenable to all, with everything else about the groups remaining separate, non-interactive, non-supportive, and often even competitive.

What if, instead, these groups had retained their identities but also merged into a lasting larger structure which wasn't the least common denominator of their "laundry lists" of concerns (the modest amount that they all could agree on) but was the greatest common sum of their agendas, that is the total of all of them combined, with no deletions? And what if each group pledged its support to the others for anything within their own domain that they undertook, accepting leadership from each other for each other's priority areas? And what if this meant that the anti-war movement, for example, would turn out support, provide person power, and even share material resources with the civil rights movement for a campaign the later initiated, and vice versa?

Take this image to the present. You still have each project, periodical, and movement. And they still function autonomously, with their own priorities in place, developing their own views and agendas. But, on top of this, they also exist within a larger structure. Let's call it SAM — the Solidarity with Autonomy Movement — for a minute.

SAM's agenda is the sum total of the agendas of all its affiliates. Its consciousness is the sum total of the consciousness of all its affiliates. Its board is composed of representatives from all its affiliates. Its budget is based on direct fund raising, as well as proportionate contributions from its affiliates. SAM in turn gives support to projects in tune with affiliate needs and potentials.

What about conflicts? Two periodicals, or projects, or movements in SAM have different views on some issue. How can such contradictory positions be held within one organization? Well, as long as becoming part of SAM is a self-conscious choice that has to be ratified by existing members, so that basic agreements are preserved and enlarged, why not? Why is this so hard? It means that there is always need for patient investigation, discussion, and assessment of differences and, in time, one hopes, progress toward more agreement. But until agreement on some controversial matter is reached, contrasting views exist and are respected in SAM. (However, in the cases of a conflict between an affiliate whose special focus is more closely related to the area of work in question and an affiliate whose focus is elsewhere, the former is given priority in SAM's program.)

There is no point pursuing all the many complex variants and possibilities of organizational arrangement, definition, and structure here. The basic image is of an umbrella organization that encompasses and includes, supportively and respectfully, a vast range of progressive and left undertakings. SAM is the greatest sum of all these affiliates. It exists to enhance each affiliate and the whole. Each affiliate understands that they have to be less purist and more willing to support a larger and therefore more diverse organization, and to live with differences. There is no presumption that one or another affiliate has all the answers. There is a presumption that all the answers that we now have are embodied within SAM as a whole, and that a mechanism for testing their worth and finding new ones, however fitfully at times, exists.

The critical first issue is who is included — what movements, projects, periodicals, and organizations? We clearly just can't say "come one, come all." There will have to be norms and structure, and new recruits will have to fit well in the eyes of those who are already affiliated. It has to be serious and committed, and each new inclusion has to be acceptable to all those already involved, to maintain levels of trust and participation.

Suppose, as but one example, representatives from the Greens, the New Party, the Labor Party, the Campaign for a New Tomorrow, and NOW got together with the purpose of creating SAM. They hammer out the structural norms — a clear understanding of what allegiance implies, a dues structure, how resources are distributed to affiliates and to overall projects, how SAM-sponsored campaigns and projects are originated, what SAM affiliates have to do vis-à-vis one another, and so on.

Then they take this vision to some other constituency groups, projects, and organizations agreeable to each of the initial groups. Perhaps they go to the *Nation*. Or perhaps they go to Greenpeace or the Institute for Policy Studies. Slowly and steadily, the growing structure could reach out to include national, regional, and even local organizing projects, periodicals, and organizations.

Would SAM include everyone who calls themselves progressive? I doubt it. But it could certainly be a very large and diverse formation, with a huge impact on solidarity and on the ability of progressive and left elements to focus their efforts effectively. Is this a pipe dream? I don't know. It seems to me that the idea of preserving the autonomy of each affiliate yet fostering solidarity among them respects both the need for unity and the need for diversity. Without some mechanism like this — some forum that can lead to a sharing of ideas, views, and agendas; to honest debate and discussion of differences; to pursuit of collective programs; to sharing of insights and merging of human support; to an enlargement of, sharing of, and sensible allocation of resources (that is, to fostering and benefiting from both solidarity and autonomy) — it seems that we are not going to go forward very far.

With some structure like SAM, however, it seems that, if not clear, the way is at least passable. The fact is, many people of good will are not doing very well right now. It's time to take a chance. As an old saying goes, there is little to lose and a whole lot to gain. Either what we have, spread across the United States in all its myriad forms, is a basis on which we can build (which I tend to believe) — in which case the SAM-type approach or something like it seems a viable and needed first step forward — or what we have is not even worth much as a starting place, and we have to create something entirely new from scratch. If that's the case, then we better figure that out sooner rather than later.

STOP WHINING,
START WINNING

Think of a professional athletic team. What distinguishes those who win from those who lose? Talent and training, of course. But let's assume talent and training are essentially the same for some set of teams. Then what distinguishes them? Luck will be a factor, of course, but I contend that it is often attitude that will be most important. Those who think they can win and who confidently approach even difficult challenges as hills to dig up and remove, or to go around, or to climb over have a chance for a great season. Those who doubt that they can win, and who despondently approach even modest challenges as immovable mountains that irremediably obstruct their way forward, have virtually no chance for even just a good season.

Imagine a successful professional football or soccer coach meeting with her team. Last weekend, they lost. Now it's time to talk about the next game or the rest of the season. Does the coach repeatedly bemoan the size and strength of the opponents? Does she talk endlessly about how the schedule is horrible for her team? Does the coach list her team's detriments and other team's strengths as if they are ordained by some athletic God and are unbridgeable impediments to success? Not likely.

The coach instead pays attention to reality, but approaches each new game from the point of view of asking what the team is in position to affect. How can the team alter their choices and behavior so as to win? If the coach spends each meeting endlessly listing the strengths of opponents without any clarification of how those strengths are to be overcome, she needs to get a new job and the team might as well take a vacation.

Now consider the left. We might not like it, but we, too, have to try to win just like professional athletic teams do. That's the currency of success in social struggle. Just playing well at improving society isn't enough. Winning ends wars, feeds the hungry, gives dignity to the exploited, and reduces their hardships. Winning can even create a new world without the need for such struggles. On the other hand, just playing nicely or "fighting the good fight" without winning, or arguably even trying to win, and instead laying the seeds for further losses to come, well, what the hell is that good for?

Does the left have a winning attitude? Can we have a good season, a good career with our current mindset? All too often the answer is no. All too often too many of us look at the half-full or quarter-full (movement) glass and we don't just see a glass that is half or three-quarters empty — which is true and needs to be recognized, of course — but we talk only about how much is missing and most especially we do so in tones that suggest that it could never be more full. Indeed, we even see leaks in the glass where they don't exist and imagine powers to deplete the glass's contents that our opponents do not have.

Too few of us ask, "How do we get more (members) into the glass, and how do we retain those we attract, rather than having them leak away?" Too often we go beyond sensibly analyzing the conditions that we encounter to whining about things that we can't influence. Too often we pay too little attention to the things about our approaches we could change so as to remove, go around, or climb over obstacles, much less mapping out agendas for doing so.

Am I exaggerating? If so, not by much. Our glass is our movements. The fact is, whether we are talking about matters of class, race, gender, political power, ecology, international relations, or whatever else, our movements aren't nearly as full of members as they need to be for us to win short-run reforms or long-run new institutions.

But how many leftists write and speak about what's wrong with society without accompanying this analysis with a strategic commentary, so that (even against our intent) it has more or less the impact of moaning about the size of next week's opponent? In contrast, how many write and speak about why our movement doesn't grow faster, or about why it loses the members who we do attract, and what we can do to have better results?

How many of us write or speak about the oppressiveness or power of the media, the state, or corporations as compared to writing or speaking about the attributes needed in our movements to oppose the media's, state's, and corporations' power and oppressiveness, and about the potential power of opposition and how it might be enhanced? And I mean "write and speak" not just in publications or at big conferences, but in our personal letters and e-mail, and especially in our face-to-face conversations.

Extending the analogy, a team or coach that doesn't know what it wants to achieve for the season will wind up wherever it is pushed by events, but not somewhere that it seeks to be, such as becoming champion. So successful teams and their coaches map out clear goals. If we are not ready to try to win the championship this year, then next year, or the next. And they attune their daily, weekly, seasonal agendas to their long-term goals.

Does the left do that? Do we have goals for the economy, the polity, for families and kinship, for the culture, for international relations, for the environment?

Do we organize our thoughts about what to do today in light not only of our current strengths and weaknesses, the immediate conditions we confront, and our immediate aims, but also in light of how all this relates to our long-term goals?

Most of the left rightly disparages professional sports for its commercialism, sexism, racism, class relations, and so on. But it would help if we learned a little from them, as well. These teams are the world's foremost competitors and, like it or not, we are in a competition, a struggle, based in class, gender, race, and political relations. Their experience reveals that if you despondently whine, you lose. On the other hand, if you confidently strategize, you have a chance to win. Likewise, if you lack goals you will wind up somewhere you would rather not be; but if you have goals, you may attain them.

This is all obvious. But it's worth repeating, and repeating again, and again. Because amid pyrotechnic displays of mental virtuosity about discoursing paradigms — as well as amid projects and movements that suffer a lack of resources and serious time pressures — the obvious is often the first thing to drop out of our consciousness.

For example, consider the Ralph Nader presidential campaign and its aftermath. During the campaign, one could have many different views about it. Sure, speeches were being given, press conferences held, rallies enjoyed, information dispersed, and so on. But to what end?

What made sense to me, as someone outside its policy-making but strongly supporting the campaign, was a multifold set of aims. The campaign should introduce good radical ideas widely into the spectrum of discussion. It should demonstrate the power of hard progressive work, and inspire it in others. It should build the Green Party and third-party organizing more generally. It should provide lessons for enhancing activism in the future. It should tally large numbers of votes as a sign of a base of committed support.

But why? One answer would be to pressure the Democratic Party — and that's it. Another would be to advance the careers or visibility and sway of certain participants, arguably. And one could imagine other unattractive possibilities. What made sense to me, however, was for people to undertake and support the campaign to increase the infrastructure and morale — and thus the power — of the left, first to win immediate reforms whether under a Gore or a Bush administration, and second to lay the groundwork for further gains in the future.

Well, what had the campaign attained just after the election? The Nader and LaDuke ticket won about 3 million votes. It attracted about 10 million people into loosely supporting it, with many of course deciding to vote for Gore as the lesser evil. There were hundreds and probably thousands of people who worked long and hard for the campaign and were invigorated by their efforts, many for the first time in their lives and others for the first time in years. And, yes, there were also a whole lot of people in the Democratic Party and in affiliated liberal organizations and institutions screaming bloody murder about Nader being a "spoiler."

So what should have been done, after the election? Well, if one sees the glass sensibly and soberly but not despondently, and has an agenda of developing the power of the left, I think we should have:

(i) solidified the activist support for the campaign into ongoing activity,

(ii) solidified the electoral support garnered by the campaign at least into lasting allegiance,

(iii) found ways to raise huge sums from that broad base of supporters to finance new projects for reaching out still further,

(iv) asked what attributes the campaign had that diminished its tally and its ability to retain support, and explored what we could do to correct these faults, and

(v) strengthened actual progressive infrastructure in the form of local, regional, and national organization, Green and otherwise.

Stop Whining, Start Winning

I think one way to work on these gains might have been to create a shadow government able to generate not only visibility but all kinds of momentum for associated outreach and participation, education, and activism. It's a little late, now, perhaps, to build on the electoral momentum, but I think it could still be very positive. But there are other ways to do so, as well, I have no doubt.

On the other hand, suppose someone thinks that the left is not a serious player in the future of our society, and that all that's really possible is tweaking existing relations this way and that. Then the agenda changes quite a lot. One has to assess one's ability to talk with elites or to create mainstream rather than dissident institutions and other such variables that are largely irrelevant from a more leftist angle.

So where is Nader in all this? I have tried to find out, but I honestly have no idea. We all know that he is largely invisible.

Nader says the media isn't paying attention. Well, that would be part of an explanation — though totally predictable and thus for the most part whiney — if he was in fact holding regular press conferences, leading demonstrations, and otherwise making serious news that ought to be covered. But I think (based on his immediate actions after the election and in the months thereafter) he isn't doing any of that. Except for some campus speaking engagements, he has been essentially quiet. Meanwhile, the momentum generated by the campaign, including his own fantastic efforts, is evaporating.

What we know hasn't happened is for the huge numbers of people involved in the campaign to develop and debate emerging views on what ought to be done; for them to urge positive actions at every level of the Green Party and to Nader, as well; for there to be open debate and discussion about urged agendas and then for there to be energy invested in forward-looking projects.

This is what a movement that believes that it can win and always tries to move forward by understanding both its gains and its need for improvement should be doing.

Has there been a time more worthy of optimism and exertion in the last 20 years? If so, not by much. Yet our movement isn't optimistic and isn't exerting energy at near the level of the campaign, much less still more energetically.

Stop Whining, Start Winning

Nader isn't doing it. Nor are the rest of us. This is a horrendous shame given the potentials that are just waiting to be galvanized into serious and lasting gains.

Can we get down to it, and by "we," I mean Ralph as well as the rest of us? Shadow government? Mass campaign for electoral reform and also substantive gains throughout social and economic life? How about a 30-hour work week? Whatever, but something rooted in clear goals and spurred by the desire and the confidence that even if it will take lots effort, in time we can win.

CLASS, RACE, SEX?

Toward the middle years of the New Left, Marxism was in the ideological saddle as activists' "systemic" guide to radical analysis. Left concepts elevated economics. Class was paramount. Imperialism was the reigning enemy. The plight of the ghettoes, the sex life of teenagers, the ills of alcoholism, the roots of crime. The astute activist's informed way into these topics or into pretty much anything else was via class categories.

Certainly some folks considered gender, sex, race, and culture — but secondarily important, or, in the technical terminology of the time, as part of the superstructure. Then along came Black Power, La Raza, the women's movement, and the gay and lesbian movements fighting not only repressive systems in society, but also reactionary residues in the left, and working to put racism, sexism, and heterosexism on the left agenda.

"Highlight our facets of society in your thought and practice," these movements instructed — not as mere derivatives, not as mere superstructure, influenced but not influential, but as critical elements in their own right.

Pay central attention to race, gender, and sexuality — not just because they profoundly impact people's lives, but as strategic keys to system maintenance and transformation.

Fast forward to today. Even with the amazing emergence of anti-globalization movements, class is, truth be told, relatively absent from the left's lexicon. Attention to the economy is not only diminished in left organizing, it is often missing entirely. Lots of leftists even celebrate markets, once a despised part of society's problems. Innovative and insightful focus on class relations, class consciousness, class struggle, and class organization is relatively slight, and has been for years. Race, gender, and sex are spotlighted.

What happened and what is to be done?

Everyone realizes that with race, gender, and sexuality added to the mix of progressive politics, many people came in who weren't high on class and anti-capitalism (just as in labor movements there are those who aren't focused on sexuality, gender, and race). But no one argues that this alone explains the decline of attention to class. After all, we should have been able to raise class consciousness for these constituencies, like we would want to raise gender, race, and sex role consciousness for labor-oriented ones, enlarging the perspective of each constituency.

So, looking for a deeper answer, some people examine this history and say that blacks, Latinos, women, and gays somehow actively pushed class out of prominence. They replaced it with all this fragmenting social stuff, and we have all paid the price. We must now gear up to reverse the trend, they argue. We must put class back on the table. In fact, to properly highlight class, we have to clear the table of exaggerated emphasis on peripheral and fragmenting concerns.

This view is now surfacing in progressive periodicals, books, and gatherings. Is it credible? According to these critics, hard upon the period of economic prioritization in the mid-1960s, attention to race (in particular, a nationalist Black Power conceptualization) came along and started the process of elbowing class aside. Then came feminists, focusing on gender. More elbowing. Then the gay movements rose and fought. Elbows flying.

Given this picture, though, I wonder why didn't the subsequent arrival of the women's movement elbow race (and not just class) off the agenda? And why didn't the arrival of queer activism elbow gender and race (and not just class) off the agenda? How come it is only class that succumbs to newly arriving prioritizations, as if the other three concerns constitute some kind of unholy alliance, when clearly they were and remain often quite at odds with each other?

If that doesn't raise any questions in your mind about the roots of the declining attention to class over the past few decades, go back and look at the rhetoric and literature of the "identity politics" movements. Were there components that largely ignored class, in some sense contributing to its diminishment? Sure. There's no sense denying it.

But why would class, previously entrenched, with a much longer pedigree, presumably so much more important in the eyes of its advocates, retreat so dramatically under such a spurious and weak assault? Moreover, consider that for every such new sector trying to *replace* class, there were others that sought to *add* race or gender or sexuality — or all of them — *to* class (and to one another), keeping class prominent and expanding left agendas.

Yes, radical feminists argued the priority of gender and kinship (in much the same way as

Class, Race, Sex?

Marxists argued the priority of class and economics) so that their battle with Marxism was, in some sense, zero sum. Again, there is no point in denying it.

But Marxist-feminists (with a hyphen) argued the need to have two conceptual toolboxes and orientations, using each in turn as appropriate. And, better still, socialist feminists (without a hyphen) saw the need to reinvent approaches to both class and gender, with each being newly informed by the other.

Socialist feminists argued for building one new conceptual toolbox with both focuses prioritized simultaneously. And while there were no comparably revealing names, the same held regarding race and sexuality and their interfaces with class.

Why, then, didn't the more insightful and innovative efforts, plus the attachment to class in the first place, keep class on the table?

That is, if class and economics were riding relatively high in the saddle and then along came efforts to put race, gender, and sex into our conceptual framework (with some elements arguing replacement but others arguing addition), how come now, 30 years later, only the advocates of class have to argue that it needs to be put back on the table. And why did class and economics fall off the table in the first place?

I think this is an interesting question and that many folks are coming to the wrong conclusions about this issue with potentially disastrous results. Yes, non-Marxist-inspired movements fought to establish the central importance of race, gender, and sexuality. But that was a needed step forward. Economism — arguing the *a priori* priority of economic relations and the superstructural subordination of kinship, cultural, sexual, and even power relations — was wrong, and would still be wrong if revived today.

So why did attention to class diminish instead of persisting alongside and entwined with other newly elevated priorities and conceptual insights?

The first broad cause of the declining attention to class by the ideological left from 1967 to now had two sides, as has been widely understood.

(i) When it was in the saddle, Marxism was like radical feminism or narrow nationalism in trying to defend a monistic prioritization of a single side of life as paramount. Marxism's advocates were wedded to this, if not always in word, certainly in most deeds. They believed it honestly and fought for it on grounds of its validity, however wrongly. Such Marxists didn't say, as they should have:

> These critics are correct in berating our economism. We have been right to be concerned about economics, but we have been wrong to think that culture, race, gender, sex, and so on are derivative.
>
> We have to welcome the criticism and incorporate the new insights. We need to expand our concepts not only of the rest of society, but even of economics, seeing how the new understandings of the emanations of influences having to do with race and gender and sex affect even the nature of capitalist economic logic and relations.

This was the mindset of the socialist feminists. It was an orientation that could have helped keep class in the movement's headlights, rather than drifting out of view.

(ii) The reason this welcoming and innovative attitude wasn't adopted by all Marxists wasn't only due to a principled if ignorant attachment to economism. It was also defensive, at least in part. That is, men in the movement and whites in the movement and straights in the movement weren't eager to have the movement challenge many of their ways and beliefs and, yes, their advantages.

So (i) and (ii) worked together to pose the problem as class *or* race, class *or* gender, class *or* sex for these Marxists.

But I don't find (i) and (ii) convincing as a full explanation of the drift away from attention to class. Yes, both these reasons were at work, but how strongly? I think a serious study would show that in fact most Marxists from the 1960s were, with some hesitation, rather open to the idea that these other concerns had to be conceptually and programmatically prioritized, not just class. I never bought that the race, gender, and sex biases of class-focused movement activists — whether we are talking their principled conceptual beliefs or their personal material and social interests — were strong enough to cause them to essentially leave the stage of social change, essentially running from the threat of race, gender, and sexual activists and thus reducing support for class politics by their absence, rather than, say, admitting the importance of other focuses and struggling on.

In fact, I think if we went back and tracked people's trajectories, we would find instead that a whole lot of these folks slowly but surely embraced race, gender, and sex politics, but also reduced their allegiances to class politics. Points (i) and (ii) just do not explain that phenomenon sufficiently, it seems to me. So what else could be at work?

I am out on a lonely limb here, but I think the additional problem which contributed to declining attention to class was that the Marxist-inspired movements advocating class focus were never very coherent in the first place. I think they left the stage largely due to their own limited allegiances.

What was the weakness of class-oriented leftism 30 years ago and how did it contribute to the drift away from class politics? Well, the old New Left was very good on ownership relations. It militantly rejected private ownership of the means of production and it understood the difference between owning capital and accumulating profits, on the one hand, and owning only one's ability to do work and selling it for wages, on the other. There were no significant confusions about any of those issues, but that was the extent of comprehension. Class meant ownership. And understanding class relations meant understanding the impact of ownership on motivations, power, and income.

That's good, but it's not good enough. The problem is that there is another locus of class definition largely left out by an exclusive prioritization of ownership relations: that is, people's relations to production per se, not just to ownership.

If one set of non-capitalists has a relative monopoly on information relevant to decision making in the workplace, on levers of economic power, on higher incomes, on more status, and another set of non-capitalists essentially enacts instructions with little access to broader information, no access to levers of decision-making power, little status, and lower incomes, this is also a difference affecting people's motivations, incentives, life conditions, and life perspectives.

This is a class division, in short, between what I call the "coordinator class" of empowered conceptual workers and the working class of more typical rote workers (skilled or not). It is not based on ownership and is, in fact, essentially invisible if the only concepts we use for discerning class difference are relations of ownership.

So what does that have to do with diminishing attention to class? Had it not been for race, gender, and sex elbowing class off the stage, perhaps the

Class, Race, Sex?

Marxist movements would have got around to this broader conceptualization. I think not. I think the answer is more or less the opposite, which is a big part of why class declined in visibility. Here's why:

(i) Marxist movements were profoundly and militantly anti-capitalist. But, at least operationally and at the level of leadership and their conceptual framework, they were pro-coordinator class, not ultimately pro-working class. The Marxist agenda was to create a new economy without private ownership, but one in which folks with a relative monopoly on information and skills bearing on decision making and on access to levers of decision-making power became the new ruling class — as in every country where Marxism has won.

(ii) Something about the arrival of race-, gender-, and sex-oriented leftism meant that if class stayed on the table, awareness of the role of the coordinator class would come to the fore.

(iii) On average (not for every Marxist, of course), this greatly weakened the resolve of Marxists to stay focused on class, causing many to fight against the new orientations, and others to align with them, but relatively few to try to keep class in focus along with race, gender, and sex.

If true, this analysis would explain events nicely. But is there anything to it? What could it be about the arrival of race, gender, and sex focuses that would have caused people paying attention to class to see beyond ownership relations to the role of information, knowledge, and monopolies on decision-making tasks in the life of coordinators and workers? Movements against racism, sexism, and heterosexism all address themselves in considerable part to the actual interpersonal social relationships between people. They look hard to find the hidden injuries of their oppressions that involve the detailed ways of relating, dismissing, and ruling one another among opposed groups.

Imagine, if you will, that the 1960s movements that highlighted class had been enlarged by adding to the class focus attention to race, gender, and sex. If class was to continue being investigated and interrogated alongside these new focuses, in short order the hidden injuries of class would surface. The methods of the newcomers — paying attention to actual social interactions, beliefs and relations, aspirations, words, and deeds — would have quickly brought to the table workers' antipathy toward lawyers, doctors, engineers, and, of course, managers. It would have led to exploration of this antipathy, revealing the basis of it in real and consistent structural economic relationships — that is, in class differences. It would have led to seeing that an economic program could oppose capital and advance either workers or coordinators, and it would therefore have led to a far more profound and needed critique of Marxism than that it was too narrow.

Working people's views of their own situations would have been heard in a context informed by the women's movement, the anti-racist movement, and the gay movements, and the concepts emerging from their views would have entered the debate and changed awareness.

Ownership would not have disappeared as a concern, to be sure. But the question of who has economic power over daily life conditions would have come to the surface, as well. The worker-capitalist interface would have stayed on the table. But the worker-coordinator interface would have joined it there, as well as concerns about race and culture broadly, gender, and sexuality.

You can see how this would have happened organically — inevitably, I think — had all the old advocates of class welcomed the new ways of thinking and the new priorities of the "social movements" and then begun to apply them to the economy, as well.

So there we have it. And what an irony. Yes, the racial and sexual biases of Marxism — whether honest intellectual errors or defenses of material and social advantages and prejudices — no doubt caused some of its members to resist new social movements and to even retire from the stage rather than persist in some new alliance that would keep class concerns prominent.

But alone, this just doesn't explain the reality. For one, why did only class decline? Two, why didn't the "add the new priorities to the old one" mentality win out over the "replace the old priorities with new ones" mentality? And, three, why did so many of the old class-focused folks actually change to embracing race, gender, and sex politics, however dropping their old prioritization?

I believe that class focus had a weak basis because:

(i) the intellectual framework and practices that sustained it were not truly committed to unequivocally pro-working class agendas, and

(ii) its advocates were highly attached to not revealing this fact even to themselves and not admitting their other class allegiance, that is, to a coordinator vision and practice, with intellectuals in command.

So what is a good way forward?

In our society, community cultural relations, gender and kinship relations, sexual relations, political power relations, and economic class relations quite evidently all powerfully determine people's life prospects. They all demarcate social groups with different circumstances, material and social interests, and prospects for becoming radicalized in various ways. Moreover, each of these spheres of social involvement and function reproduce not only their own defining oppressive hierarchies, but due to having been molded by the others so powerfully, contribute to all the defining oppressive hierarchies.

To understand any aspect — economy, kinship, community, polity — requires concepts fully informed by lessons from examining the others. Yes, we need to put class back on the activist agenda. We need class concepts organizing our perceptions and structuring our thoughts. We need class vision providing aspirations and orientation, and class strategy to guide our practical choices. But we also need gender, race, and sexual concepts, vision, and strategy. We need a way to practice politics that respects the autonomy of the constituencies all these aspects of life define and that gives each room to develop and nurture its own agendas, and which simultaneously breaks down the biases of each against real solidarity.

If we go from having had class in the saddle of a one-horse show to having race, gender, and sex in three saddles of three horses running largely at odds with each other, and then back to the one-horse class myopia again, it will pile shame and error upon shame and error.

Dump the horses entirely. Dump the either/or mentality about what is important in social life and strategy.

Create a conceptual framework that pays proper regard to all critical sides of social life, in particular to economics, polity, culture, and kinship. Create movements that combine the needed autonomy of issue-focused projects and movements that will emerge and are needed for their constituencies to find their own agendas, and the solidarity that is prerequisite for any one agenda to be fully informed by essential insights from all the others.

Sure, the arguments involve more than two steps. But it isn't rocket science. It's as clear as the world around us, and has been for decades now. And while we are at it — expand our class concepts to account for the three-class, rather than two-class, environment we operate within.

A friend of mine told me one day of saying to his three-year-old child, "You can do this, or you can do that. Now, let's get on with it. Which will it be." And the child said back, "But, daddy, I don't like either choice."

Three year olds can manage this level of comprehension. We don't have to choose between class myopia and non-class myopia. This time around, surely we can opt for something broader than these competing failed orientations. If we don't, we have only ourselves to blame.

MY GENERATION

I think that we 1960s radicals have done a pretty poor job of communicating with the next generation about a lot of issues. I say that because I encounter a lot of young people who feel that they're transcending the ills of the 1960s — which would be a good thing, if it were true. It would be a very good thing indeed to transcend the ills of the time, but actually very often they are reproducing them. The real ills of the 1960s, or least many of the real ills, are rarely labeled as such.

One of the kinds of ills that we had was something called sectarianism. Sectarianism is generally thought to arise from automatic reflex adherence to a perspective. But that's not an adequate explanation. It seems to me that, in practice at least, one of the things that has a great deal to do with sectarianism is somehow connecting your personal identity to a set of ideas, so that if anybody challenges something that you think, it is taken as this devastating attack upon your being.

People tend to equate themselves with the current ideas that they have, and if somebody says they disagree with those ideas, it is taken as equivalent to saying, "You're a schmuck. You're a fool. You're an idiot. You're a decrepit slob, because I disagree with a belief you have."

So then the ideas have to be defended in the same way that one would defend one's soul, because the ideas have become entwined with one's soul. But that's not the way we ought to defend ideas. Souls deserve that kind of defense, and perhaps human personalities do, too, but not ideas.

I don't think young people have understood that about ideas because I don't think it has been conveyed well. It's not something that's easy to convey.

It's a lot harder to convey than the insight that U.S. corporations are going to control job opportunities, or the state will operate to repress movements, and so on. That's easy. These more experiential lessons are harder to convey, and my generation hasn't done a very good a job of it.

Another idea that we haven't conveyed well, especially to young people, is about another way we went wrong. There's a tendency philosophers call a slippery slope. We take what we do, and always push it to some kind of an extreme. We see some good idea, and then we take it to this fantastic extreme in which we reduce the original value of the idea or even make it counterproductive.

The way we understand consumerism is an example. The slope goes sort of like this. Consumerism is a bad thing. Consumerism involves a degree of advertising manipulation. Consumerism means that people have been tricked. Consumerism means people are fools and therefore we shouldn't consume.

You see how we're slowly going down a slope in which we have taken an insight, that consumerism (whatever that might be) is bad, and instead of refining it and benefiting from it, we have made it so extreme that it literally gets in the way of existence. In fact, it's impossible to live if you don't consume. Yet we come to this view that everybody who consumes more than some minimum is a fool and has been tricked.

This is not a good slope to go down. And this is just one of many that we go down where we take good initial insights — there are bad technologies, reforms can be cooptive, institutions can delimit our options, and so on — which are, however, very incomplete and partial, and take them so far that they are no longer valuable. Thus we end up with the view that technology per se is bad, or that seeking reforms is inevitably selling out, or that we should reject all institutions.

Another thing that we came up with — or, more specifically, that the women's movement came up with — was a recognition that "the personal is political." This was a very powerful insight 30 years ago. "The personal is political" then meant something very different from what I think many people now think it means.

"The personal is political" meant that there are many things in people's personal lives that have political causes and dimensions that are wider than the individual. So, "the personal is political" meant rape, something personal, is political. Battering, something personal, is political. For that matter, poverty, something personal, is political. Racial hatred, something personal, is political.

These were valuable insights. But it if we start down the associated slippery slope, "the personal is political" can get exaggerated, can be distorted, and eventually can come to mean almost the opposite of what was intended, that the *essence* of politics is personal. The meaning has been almost exactly reversed, so that now we begin to have the feeling that everything is a function of personal, individual, totally separate, totally atomized choices.

Do we or do we not consume? Do we or do we not use lipstick? Do we or do we not smoke, or eat meat, or watch TV? Politics loses its collective and strategic impetus and we drown in interpersonal judgmentalism.

This trend is partially embodied in many sides of contemporary thought and activism, not least, for example, in elements of what are called "third-wave feminism," "identity politics," "food politics," "lifestyle politics," and so on. The problem is twofold. First, this type of approach generates a highly judgmental mindset in which each individual begins to see her or his own choices as superior and those of anyone who chooses differently as inferior. Second, this type of approach denigrates what ought to be primary: people grouping together into collective shared struggle for change.

Something went wrong with the slogan "speak truth to power," too. "Speak truth to power" does not mean try and convince power by the logic of your truth. If it means that, it's a slogan we should dump, because power doesn't listen to logic. Power doesn't give a damn about truth. The phrase just meant stand up with the truth and assert your-self with it. But somehow it got screwed up into "speak truth *to* power." Spend a lot of time trying to convince power of what the truth is. But that's a total waste of time. Power only responds to raising social costs, to force, basically.

How do we know what we each ought to be doing? A lot of people in my generation sort of beat themselves up answering this question. Some-body figures out that it's a good idea to be a com-munity organizer. It's a good idea to be a labor organizer. It's a good idea to go into the police and organize the police. It's a good idea to organize whatever it is. And then everybody has to do that. Because that's the right thing to do. Do the right thing. That's the right thing.

But what if some people aren't very well dis-posed to do the thing that was just mentioned? What if it just doesn't fit their personality, charac-ter, traits, or skills? That goes by the wayside and the people beat themselves up to do the thing that's at the top of the list of important things on that day — a list which keeps rotating, by the way. That's a horrible mistake.

My Generation

When I say that today's youth are repeating our errors, I mean they are repeating mistakes like that. It seems to me that we should have conveyed the understanding that revolution isn't apocalyptic. It doesn't happen tomorrow. It's a long process. One has to be in it for the long haul, and one has to carve out a space in which one can function, be productive, and live a life. Even if it isn't revolution, even if you just believe in making the system less oppressive, the same thing holds. You have to carve out a spot in which it's possible to function and to be effective.

That means you don't just do what somebody else says is most important. You do things that you can do. You do things that will sustain you. We're each different, and so we have to figure out where we fit. Not according to some abstract pronouncement that "it is now proper to go into such-and-such type of community and be such and such type of organizer." If that's not who we are, we won't do a good job. In fact, we'll do a crummy job and we won't last long.

There's another slogan that came out of the period when my political activism was born. That was the slogan "dare to struggle, dare to win."

That's not from here in the United States but from China. I don't know what it meant in China, but I assume it meant what I take it to mean here. And it seems to me that it's a very wise slogan. It actually is a very profound and wise little instruction. It doesn't make much sense, on the face of it. Why would you have to dare to struggle and, in particular, why would you have to dare to win? It's because you don't have any confidence in yourself. It's because you don't believe that, in fact, you can do anything any better. You don't believe in yourself, or we don't believe in ourselves. And there is really a lot of insight in that, I think.

For some, "dare to struggle, dare to win" translates into the slogan, now Americanized, "we are the leaders we've been looking for." These are not trivial notions. In many ways, they are more profound and they embody more wisdom than an analysis of how U.S. corporations work, or patriarchy works, or racism works, or authority works — not least because understanding these issues alone doesn't necessarily help you become an effective, powerful, lasting organizer.

SUSTAINING RADICALISM

As folks comprehend society and begin to think about alternatives and strategies, why are some people revolutionaries?

On the one hand, we're revolutionaries because we look at the world and we see the horrors described earlier in this book and many more, and we react. We decide we are going to be revolutionary because we can't abide institutions that oppress people as their basic logical outcome. Among people who I've talked to who see themselves as revolutionaries, one or more of the following five reasons seem to be operating.

One is to do the right thing.

Another is to improve one's own life, literally to improve one's situation in the world.

Another reason is out of solidarity for others, which is not the same as acting out of self-interest.

Another is because it's fun. That is, because it's a better life.

And another is to win.

Being a revolutionary to do the right thing is based on an ethical argument, the ethical and the moral desire to be a revolutionary. The good side of this approach is that you are self-conscious about your ethics and your behavior. The bad part of this is that you don't have to be strategic. You don't have to try to win. You don't even have to try to accomplish much of anything. You're doing it to do the right thing.

If this motivation is operating alone, you often encounter an individual who says they're revolutionary and they are doing the right thing by opposing injustice. They're trying to be moral, but they aren't thinking about how to be effective.

Suppose you are revolutionary to improve your personal life. That's obviously good, especially if you happen to be in a position in society where improving your personal life is part and parcel of what really is making a revolution. But this motivation can also be very narrow. The idea that the only thing that we can comprehend is our own exact situation and our own narrow position in the world is a very debilitating one. It is possible to understand somebody else's pain and suffering at least enough to empathize with it and try and overcome it. So, while it's necessary to be concerned about overcoming the forms of oppression one endures directly, it isn't sufficient. If we don't have solidarity with others, we'll never have movements that cross hierarchies and focuses.

Trying to revolutionize society because it is fun is no joke. That is to say, if social change isn't fun, the probability that people will keep trying to do it through hard times and over the long haul is vastly reduced. So, it's actually important that people are engaged in activism because it's preferable to doing other things, which means again that we need a movement that does not involve perpetually going through a gauntlet of debilitating criticism that makes us feel rotten.

Not that we can't be critical when appropriate, but we can't allow life in the movement to be so depressing that it's worse than working in a factory. Life in the movement can't be more boring, more negating, than life out in the real world. If we have a movement like that, what is the probability that it's going to win?

The last reason to be a revolutionary is to win. I very rarely meet people in the United States who honestly think we can win. This is a very severe problem. It is very difficult to try to do something when you don't think you can do it. It may be possible, barely, but it is certainly very difficult.

I think people need to ask themselves if they really think they can win. If they want to be a revolutionary, then they have to think long and hard about some scenario that gives them some feeling of potential success. Why do people stay in this business of trying to change the world year after year after year, including in difficult times? Broadly, there are only two reasons. One is religious, in a sense, and the other is strategic.

If you look back in the early part of this century at the people who were revolutionary out of a religious conviction, they were still in the thick of it 30 or 40 years later. Somehow their beliefs provide the sustenance that lets them stay in the struggle whether they think they're going to win or not.

The other group of people who stay in the struggle for the long haul understand the process. They see the victories, and they see the gains. They see the losses, too, but they can comprehend them rather than being motivationally destroyed by them. They can deal with the feelings of depression and of difficulty, not out of faith, but out of understanding. It's not that they're immune to frustration and depression. Even great and seemingly tireless organizers aren't immune to such feelings.

Sustaining Radicalism

They have those feelings just like anybody else does, but at some level they understand something about the world that gives them the ability to get past these frustrations and to feel hope.

WHAT ARE WE WAITING FOR?

Our commitment to ultimately revolutionize all aspects of life should affect how our immediate campaigns are defined, what immediate goals we seek, and how we seek these goals. It should inform what we talk about when we organize, write, speak, and teach — what ideas we try to convey, what commitments we try to elicit. This is what seems missing from progressive and left activism, and from our very lives, today.

The absence of unifying goals, of shared long-term commitment, and of attention to communicating these forthrightly at every opportunity weakens not only our prospects of organizing usefully toward a distant end, but also our near-term efforts to reduce pain today. Today's activism, for want of revolutionary designs and spirit, is often ill-informed, frequently lacks integrity, and virtually never incorporates the kind of logic, solidarity, and spirit that can sustain long-term involvement by suffering constituencies.

Current movements are most often too narrow, too lacking in scope and in spiritual and moral appeal to attract wide support. Remarkably, they often celebrate their very weaknesses, their lack of vision, their lack of breadth, and their lack of anything resembling audacity and passion as if these debits were virtues.

At the level of feeling, of emotion, and of consciousness, our projects often do little to overcome (and sometimes even contribute to) the main hesitancy that impedes most people today from taking a progressive stand: the belief that nothing significantly better than what America offers is logically possible. Or, even if it is logically possible, the belief that certainly nothing significantly better than what we endure can actually be attained — so why bother?

Our projects rarely convey a broad understanding of systemic causes of problems and almost never offer positive institutional alternatives to the status quo that can provide hope and motivation. From the outside (and often from the inside too), our efforts look just like or sometimes even worse than the status quo, so they are generally powerless to address the average citizen's deep-seated cynicism.

A left worth joining in the United States today should be fighting vigorously for immediate gains that can alleviate suffering and advance a degree of immediate dignity and justice for people, of course. We should be trying to win a 30-hour work week with full pay, full employment, real affirmative action, a comprehensive housing program, a humane health care program, a rich preschool and public education program, a real living wage, electoral reforms that empower disenfranchised constituencies, a non-intrusive foreign policy, workers' and community rights over corporate greed, and many other reforms.

We should communicate not only how these changes are each good in their own right, but how they gain immensely when linked together as part of a process of developing movements and organizations capable of attaining a new society whose broad character we need to be able to lay out in clear and reasonably concise language, and whose details we need to evolve through our practice.

Once one has understood even the most elementary truths about capitalism, patriarchy, racism, and authoritarianism, as so many of us have at one time or another in our lives, I don't see how less than the above is honest, just, or strategic. Optimistically, I also think the public is more ready than it has been in decades for a movement that clearly and passionately offers long-term vision and commitment, as well as immediate short-term benefit.

So what are we waiting for?

We need to replace all the timidity, the defensiveness, the worry about being thought juvenile or irresponsible that has grown since the 1960s with bold, honest, forthright statements of what is oh so obviously true, now as before.

This country needs a revolution, the most profound and broad revolution in history, and people of good will and clear vision need to be working for it. People need to be working on vision, on strategy, on program, on building alliances and organizations, on winning immediate reforms and parlaying them into greater power to win still more gains in a continuing trajectory of struggle, now and hereafter. We need to know what we want. And we need to live and fight for it. Entirely.

URGENT PATIENT TASKS

The architect wants to be able to predict future changes in architectural insights. The militarist wants to anticipate the construction of future weapons. The mathematician wants to extrapolate future theorems. The musician wants to conceive of future compositional styles. The engineer wants to conceptualize future mechanical and electrical innovations.

Their motive? If they can confidently envision future innovations, they can get in on the ground floor. They can do today what will enhance tomorrow. They can avoid squandering time on efforts that come to naught.

The same holds for foreseeing the insights and methods that will characterize more successful future activist movements. Envisioning where future activists will make great and important progress can help us today.

In the future, when the left is growing and succeeding more widely, we can predict that it will have a popularly formulated, widely held, substantial, and compelling vision dealing with the main areas of social life in ways that inspire people, provide hope, shape long-term strategy, and inform a short-term program.

"What are you for?" people constantly ask us. It is a fair question. We shouldn't defend not having accessible, shared answers. We shouldn't justify lack of vision as reflecting the difficulty of envisioning. We ought to acknowledge that not having vision is a serious problem. We ought to realize that since having vision will be part of having stronger movements in a desirable future, the time to develop vision is now.

Today, people know that the basics of society are broken. People also know that various ills are social and not personal, systemic and not private. But people don't know what to do about it.

If we don't talk about vision and strategy with a breadth and depth that meet people's doubts, then we aren't addressing the most powerful obstacle to people actively seeking change: their doubt that change is possible, much less that we can induce change by our efforts, much less that they themselves personally can usefully contribute.

To undercut people's fatalist, crippling belief that there is no better alternative than what we endure, we need compelling enunciation of the features of better alternatives, experiments in enacting those features, and victories that bring us nearer to their generalized enactment.

People need a left that not only enumerates the ills of the suffering system everyone already sees and feels, but one that also provides hope and direction by addressing questions like:

"What do we want?"

"How do we get it?" and

"What can I do that will matter?"

As we activists keep highlighting the causes and features of problems around us and clarifying confusions induced by media manipulations, here are some additional intellectual tasks that are critically important to reaching an optimistic future.

(i) Develop gender/kinship vision.

Activists rightly seek affirmative action and other reforms to restrain sexist tendencies. But what about creating new institutions that produce positive kinship and gender outcomes? What institutions can accomplish procreation, nurturance, and socialization in ways that propel broader feminist aims?

If we feel that every worthy gain that we achieve — changes in voting, in payment levels, in media representations, in medical treatment, in reproductive rights — risks being sundered by a return to the past that eats away at hard-fought victories, it is hard to keep fighting for the gains. But if we feel that every gain is part of a discernible road to a new future, we will have anticipation and hope that will fuel ongoing struggle.

Certainly, we need a vision for what families should look like, how parenting can be carried out without reinforcing sexist gender roles, how children and parents can play meaningful roles in communities — not just in circumscribed nuclear family units — and how we can develop institutions that encourage a diversity of family arrangements capable of meeting a wide range of needs.

We need to understand sexuality as a form of human expression (not just as procreation) that we should support and celebrate in all its diversity.

We need to look at how we regard and reward work outside the home versus work inside the home. Sexist workplace practices, the lack of comparable worth for women's work, welfare and child care policies that punish women's independence, and a socioeconomic system that makes invisible caretaking work all devalue women. This in turn supports the dehumanization of women in other areas of life.

Feminists have long criticized sexist institutions. But how would we replace them with ones that support liberatory gender relations, sexual practice, and caretaking?

Since having a gender-related vision will be part of successful future movements, shouldn't it become a priority focus of feminist organizations, writers, and activists now?

(ii) Develop cultural and community vision.

We rightly seek affirmative action and other reforms to restrain and then reverse racist tendencies. But what about attaining new institutions that produce positive cultural outcomes vis-à-vis race, religion, ethnicity, and national allegiances?

What institutions can facilitate people creating, elaborating, and enjoying modes of celebration, communication, mutual recognition, moral development, and cultural identity in ways that enhance rather than subvert the cultural values we hold dear?

How can people have cultural communities to sustain and advance their lives without pitting those communities against one another?

Multiculturalism — and what movements of the late 1960s called intercommunalism — already highlights targets for opposition, as well as some positive aims. But, beyond communities respecting one another, a future with successful social movements will certainly have clear, cogent enunciations of the causes of the hierarchicalization of religious, ethnic, racial, and national communities; positive aims for defensively holding these bitter causes in check; and proposals for new structures that promote true cultural diversity and solidarity among communities.

So, doesn't developing such visionary insights about religion, race, ethnicity, nationality, and other cultural community relations and making the insights public and widespread warrant priority attention?

How else can we move toward the better cultural future we anticipate?

(iii) Develop political vision.

Social activists rightly fight for new laws all the time. For example, many work to enlarge enfranchisement and to expand democratic rights or eliminate residual violations of them. But beyond specific political gains, how can society accomplish political functions in a way that is compatible with political values that we hold dear?

In a better future, we will work toward ways to legislate, adjudicate disputes, address violations of citizens' rights, and arrive at and implement shared projects so we not only reach good outcomes and justice in each particular instance but encourage larger social trends that foster equity, honesty, diversity, sociability, participation, and true democracy. If we will have such shared institutional goals in the not-too-distant future, doesn't it make sense to begin elaborating and refining them now?

We don't want vast differences in power. That is obvious and has been an inspiring anarchist credo for a century and more. But beyond that broad aim, we need convincing substance able to inspire hope and inform strategy.

Clearly, successful future movements will know what they want vis-à-vis judicial affairs, law making, and realization of shared political programs. So, isn't it about time movements in the present developed and then widely refined and shared such aims, preparing for that more effective future?

(iv) Develop economic vision.

We don't want economic institutions that array actors against one another, homogenize options, create wide differentials in circumstances or income, or misappropriate influence over choices so that a few people rule and many obey.

We don't want class division and class rule making our workplaces into dictatorships of owners and managers who determine outcomes and enjoy rewards over and above working people.

We don't want vicious competition, poverty, pollution, alienation, and subservience.

But what do we want in place of markets, private ownership, and corporate workplace organization?

How will we remunerate people, if not based on power and property? How should economic decisions be made, and by whom? What institutions should we seek for economic life?

Envision huge numbers of working people seeking massive alterations in economic life, hopefully in the not-too-distant future. Surely such a robust workers' movement will have clearly enunciated and publicly shared economic vision. It will have a convincing and inspiring vision that is refined, popularized, and made relevant to people's program and strategy, to their ways of arguing, and to their reasons for hope.

I believe participatory economics provides such an economic vision, but whether it does or not, the fact that we now need to develop economic vision is beyond dispute.[1] So among all our other priorities, shouldn't at least some of us — probably quite a few of us — be doing so?

(v) Develop an international relations vision.

There are huge movements around the world opposing the World Bank, the IMF, and the WTO. They oppose not globalization, but efforts to pervert global ties at the expense of the weak and poor in order to enhance the power and wealth of the already hugely powerful and immensely wealthy. There are also movements against war and other violations of cultural, economic, and social exchange among nations.

But what is the positive alternative? What institutions should mediate international exchange, trade, and culture to enhance equity, diversity, solidarity, and participation with appropriate influence over decisions?

Really effective "anti-globalization movements" and international peace and justice movements are going to be able to enunciate vision for international relations and fight for changes attaining the new relations.

If that is so, shouldn't we be working out such international relations aims, trying to develop popular support for them to speed the whole process?

(vi) Develop ecological vision.

For decades, substantial numbers of people have focused on ecological and environmental matters. In part, they have worked to protect humanity from egregious violations of nature that rebound to our disadvantage. In part, they have worked to protect other species and aspects of nature in their own right. These ecology movements have emphasized sustainability and caretaking, among other values.

We know we don't want despoiled rivers, befouled air, poisoned water supplies, depleted forests, or species annihilation. But what are our positive aspirations? What ecological institutional structures and practices do we favor? Surely powerful future activism on behalf of ecological sanity and innovation will have goals, so shouldn't we begin generating and sharing them in the present?

(vii) Develop strategic concepts and plans.

Urgent Patient Tasks

People ask activists not only what do you want, but how do you expect to get it against the immense obstacles in your way? This is also a fair question.

Explaining the tremendous power of existing institutions, describing their many tentacles and interconnections, and charting their pervasive influence and tenacity does not provide an answer.

We need to compellingly describe a strategic path forward. We need to explain the range of demands, infrastructure, projects, issues, and tactics regarding kinship, culture, politics, economics, international relations, and ecology that will together comprise a trajectory of change to a better future.

We need to show how the visionary aims that we advocate and an array of proposed organizational programs and tactics that we implement in the present can combine into a confident forward-moving trajectory of change that people refine by their accumulating experience.

We need to:

(a) Clarify who we are organizing, in what forms of movement and organization, with what programs, and employing what tactics for outreach and communication.

(b) Describe the kinds of organizational structure that can empower activism and lead toward the visions we seek.

(c) Refine our understanding of what wins immediate reforms, and of what "non-reformist reforms" we need to be winning to string together a convincing, non-reversible trajectory of change.

We know that broad understanding of these strategic matters will characterize a viable, powerful, left movement in the future. So, doesn't it make sense to start producing that understanding now?

•

When we talk about globalization, or racism, or war, or abuse of women, children, or gays, or poverty, or media control, or any other ugly dimension of contemporary life, shouldn't we be rooting our discussion in long-term positive aims and proposing means to win victories that improve lives now but also move toward those longer term aims?

If the answer is no, fine. Then we are already doing okay.

But if the answer is yes, then look through archives of left writing and judge critically whether we are doing enough of this already. And if we aren't doing enough of it, let's do more.

The simple organizational task list associated with the above intellectual task list is to build vision and strategy in deeds and not just thoughts. It entails beginning cautiously and realizing that the details will become clearer as we proceed. But we can usefully detail some specific steps.

(i) Clean up our existing institutions and projects.

Movements in the future will reflect our values rather than replicate the oppressions of the social structures we oppose. Shouldn't we bring the day closer by working to make it so?

Progressive and left activists are all for ending racism and sexism in society. We know that we must also persevere to reduce and finally end racial and sexual hierarchies inside our movements. Otherwise we are hypocritical, uninspiring, and will suffer the ills of these oppressions ourselves. Moreover, our movements will not attract or retain women and people of color, nor effectively pursue our anti-racist and anti-sexist priorities.

There is more work to be done around issues of race and gender in our movement organizations, but the insight is good and the activity is pointing in the right direction.

However, progressive and left activists are also for ending economic injustice and class hierarchy in society. And we have to realize that we must patiently, calmly, and constructively restructure our movements so that they no longer replicate corporate divisions of labor and decision making, as well as market norms of remuneration.

This must become a priority if we are to transcend hypocrisy, become inspiring, escape class alienation ourselves, attract, retain, and empower working people in our efforts, and achieve economic justice. Class, which once crowded race and gender off our agendas, now needs to be brought back in as a priority — in ways that address not only the ills of capital, but those of high-level decision-makers and mind workers, too, and, that elevate the positive needs of labor.

Envision a future with left advances and innovations, even well short of complete victories. Surely our left movements will embody our values and our organizations will be congenial to our primary constituencies. So knowing that is the future, shouldn't attaining it be a priority of the present?

Urgent Patient Tasks

The left has a great many research organizations, think tanks, media projects, and organizing centers. In principle, we know that these should manifest our values in their internal organization. We know they will do so in a future time when we are making great progress. They will then provide a worthy model. Working in them we will learn the implications of our aims in practice. They will be congenial to us whatever our backgrounds.

We all know this will be the case sometime down the road. We even abide by these ideals to a considerable extent in our own current practice — as we work hard to eliminate racial and gender hierarchies in our work. And that's to the good.

The problem still to be addressed is to incorporate into our projects desirable norms and values regarding class. When our current organizations pay people, they most often do it according to classist norms, rewarding power and position.

When our organizations have job responsibilities, these are most often marked by hierarchies of fulfillment and empowerment attributes quite like those typical in capitalist corporations.

Some of our people work in offices, make decisions, get higher pay, and have more status. Others of our people work more menially, are obedient, have less or no status, and earn much less pay and have much less power, as well. The main donor or fund raiser often dominates decisions in our institutions.

In short, rather than reducing class divisions by providing jobs that employ people's full capacities and share onerous tasks equitably, our organizations are marked by typical corporate relations.

We know that in the future our institutions will embody our positive race and gender, and also our positive economic values. So the associated task we face is to continue to improve our attention to race and gender in our movements, and to seriously initiate and expand our attention to matters of class, as well — creating a movement environment seeking to internally eliminate class division rather than a movement environment that replicates the larger society's class structure and, in so doing, is hostile to working-class involvement.

(ii) Develop a new encompassing structure to combine our many activisms in solidarity even while also respecting their autonomy.

Movements elevate different priorities because people endure different conditions depending on race, gender, class, sexuality, and diverse other factors. This is an inevitable fact of life. It is not going to disappear. The ensuing diversity of orientation is to the good in the breadth and depth of attention it gives each side of life.

On the other hand, that our movements often don't aid one another, or that they even compete with one another, is bad. This dynamic robs each movement of the unity with others that is essential to its success. We can confidently predict that in the future, when our movements are more successful, this atomization won't be our lot. There will be diverse focuses, yes, but there will also be mutual trust, learning, and solidarity.

Different agendas need space to develop, gain confidence, and retain focus. But to win, different agendas also need a breadth of allegiance, which means that each has to benefit from the strength and character of the rest.

So we know that some time in the future we will solve the problem of respecting diversity and autonomy even as we also find ways to have an overarching sense of solidarity.

That being so, shouldn't we address the problem sooner rather than later? Everyone will ultimately be fighting the totality of oppressions, mutually supportively, even as they may focus more on one or another.

One big step in this direction will be for larger movements to support smaller ones, and for richer ones to help pay the way of poorer ones — unreservedly and with people's bodies and resources, too. This is a project worth working on now.

(iii) Develop means to communicate widely, not only reaching those looking for our messages, but reaching the broader populace not yet in tune, as well.

It is a constant refrain — "How come you leftists are always talking to the choir?" There are no doubt some folks who do it because it is easier than reaching out to people we don't know who may disagree with what we have to say, who may even be hostile at times. Folks with this insular attitude ought to rethink it, of course.

But the main explanation for why people on the left are most often talking to people who are also on the left, or who already wish to be on the left, is that the left doesn't have a megaphone that we can shout into that is loud enough to be heard by folks who aren't already all ears to our messages.

Our media are still very small so that even when we bust a gut shouting, we reach overwhelmingly only folks who are already listening for us.

Envision a future, more successful movement. Surely one aspect will be that has the means to communicate with the broad population. That being so, why not move in that direction starting now?

We need to strengthen our current alternative media, supporting and enlarging it, and we need to pressure mainstream media, as well. But beyond those two tasks we also need to take seriously the problem of how the left gains mass media mechanisms that place left views, analyses, agendas, and visions in the face of the whole population rather than appearing only in hard-to-find nooks and crannies that people have to search for to even know that we exist.

This will happen sooner if we begin taking it seriously now rather than later.

(iv) Develop means to finance operations consistent with our values and aspirations.

Look down the road at future movements. They will still have bills to pay. They must amass appropriate funds. They will do it, surely, and in ways consistent with democratic, accountable, and equitable norms. So why not move in such directions starting now?

There is a very odd condition in our movements. We know that money matters in our societies, but we don't seem to realize that money matters on the left, too. Where does it come from? How is it handled? Is it empowering a few to the detriment of the many? Is there enough of it?

Most leftists don't know the answers because this topic is essentially taboo. Try to find essays and ruminations much less proposals about how events, projects, and demos should be funded, much less about how funds that come in should be redistributed among efforts. Mostly, you can't.

There is a gigantic silence.

Here's but one example, not the biggest, but currently on my mind. There is endless talk on the left about using the Internet constructively, which is good, but there is almost no talk about how to have left Internet operations generate revenues.

Maybe this focus should be called the Ostrich Problem. Ignoring how we get and handle money is a dead-end approach, beneficial only to those who monopolize control of what marginal monies the left now enjoys. This problem also needs to be addressed if were are going to see a future with more effective movement activism.

(v) Develop movements that will retain their members.

Envision future movements. Surely they are entities that will inspire, empower, fill needs, raise aspirations, enrich lives. Surely, once people come within their orbit, they will stay.

Yet, over the past few decades, millions of folks have come into proximity of the left, participated in various events and projects, but later opted out. There are many reasons why people often don't stick with political dissent and activism. Not least, a movement that can persevere over the long haul with continuity and commitment needs to uplift rather than to harass its membership, to enrich its members' lives rather than to diminish them, to meet its members' needs rather than to neglect them. To join a movement and become more lonely is not conducive to movements growing. To join a movement and laugh less doesn't yield ever larger and more powerful movements.

Thus, to be on the road to the future, rather than marking time going nowhere desirable, we need to organize projects that folks from all kinds of backgrounds would want to spend their time participating in, even if doing so weren't the moral and socially responsible thing to do.

It isn't that changing the world can become all play and no work. Movement building involves lots of tedium and hard work, of course. But there is no reason to make our movement building as deadening as possible, rather than as rich, varied, and rewarding as possible.

Movement participation should provide people full, diverse lives that real people can take part in, not merely long meetings or obscure lifestyles so divorced from social involvement that they preclude all but a very few people from joining.

We struggle to make the world less oppressive and more liberating. Doing the same for our movements is part of the same project.

We know this achievement will occur, that future movements will be "sticky" movements in which people who come into contact with us will stay committed to our long-term goals. So, we ought to get on about solving the problem now.

Notes

1   For more on participatory economics, see the Parecon web site at http://www.parecon.org.

AFTERWORD

As I complete my review of the manuscript of this volume, so ably chosen and edited by South End's Anthony Arnove from a much more amorphous manuscript, all written well before September 11, 2001, it seems only proper to add some statement, some acknowledgement, some comment, some primal scream, regarding what primarily occupies my mind at this time: the ongoing U.S. assault on Afghanistan and the projected "war on terrorism."

Rather than write something contrived to fit perfectly here, however, I think it is better to honestly show how the sentiments throughout this volume informed a specific essay written about the ongoing war. This is only one of many essays I provided on the events of 9/11 and after, which can all be accessed on-line on the Znet web site (http://www.zmag.org). This particular essay was called "What's So Complex About It?" Unlike various others that I wrote, often with co-author Stephen Shalom, which were more sober and meant for a wider audience, I have to admit that I was venting in this piece, and trying to communicate with folks well along the paths outlined in this volume. Thus:

The U.S. bombing of Afghanistan is a barbaric assault on defenseless civilians. It threatens a nearly incomprehensible human calamity. It is pursuing abominable goals.

The bombing is not a "just war," as Richard Falk labels it in *The Nation,* but a vigilante attack.[1] No, it is not a vigilante attack; it is a vigilante lynch-mob assault writ large. No, it is not even a vigilante lynch-mob assault writ large — even vigilante lynch mobs go after only those they think are culprits and not innocent bystanders.

The bombing of Afghanistan is a gargantuan repugnance hurled against some of the poorest people on the planet. And this gargantuan repugnance is undertaken not out of sincere if horrendously misguided desires to curtail terrorism — since the bombing undeniably manifests terror and feeds the wellsprings of more terrorism to come — but out of malicious desires to establish a new elite-serving logic of U.S. policymaking via an endless "war on terrorism" to replace the defunct Cold War. This is rehashed Reaganism made more cataclysmic than even Reagan's dismal mind could conceive.

When people ask, "But doesn't the United States have a right to defend itself? Don't we have to do something?" I understand their hurt, pain, anger, and confusion. But I also have to admit that I want to scream that the United States is increasing the likelihood that a million or more souls will suffer fatal starvation. That is not self-defense. "Doing something" does not entail that we be barbaric. We can do something desirable rather than horrific, for example.

Put differently, what kind of thinking sees denying food to humans as self-defense, as the only "something" at our disposal? The answer is thinking like Bush's, thinking like bin Laden's, thinking that treats innocent human lives as chess pieces, as checkers, in the pursuit of its own deadly agendas. Thinking that is willing to rocket a plane into a building to take 3,000 innocent lives, or thinking that is willing to drop bombs into an already devastated country, abetting cataclysmic starvation, is terrorist thinking.

Or, more often, in the case of average upset folks, it is thinking that has been systematically denied the most basic information relevant to the issues at hand. Thinking that is too fearful, depressed, angry, or cynical to admit disturbing truths and reason through real options and values.

You think I exaggerate?

Jean Ziegler, Special Rapporteur on the Right to Food to the U.N. High Commissioner for Human Rights, said on October 15, 2001, "The bombing has to stop right now."

Lest anyone miss the point, he continued, "Winter is coming in two weeks and aid convoys won't be able to reach people in Afghanistan." Ziegler also called the bombing "a catastrophe for humanitarian aid" in Afghanistan.[2]

A spokesperson for the United Nations High Commissioner for Refugees, said: "We are facing a humanitarian crisis of epic proportions in Afghanistan with 7.5 million short of food and at risk of starvation."[3]

Or in the words of Christian Aid's Dominic Nutt (quoted in *The Scotsman* but in no U.S. papers):

> We are beyond the stage where we can sit down and talk about this over tea. If they stop the bombing we can get the food aid in, it's as simple as that. Tony Blair and George Bush have repeatedly said this is a three-stringed offensive — diplomatic, military and humanitar-

ian. Well the diplomatic and military are there but where is the humanitarian? A few planes throwing lunchboxes around over the mountains is laughable.[4]

You can look at reports from one aid agency after another. It is all the same story: there's an impending calamity. Stop the bombing.

So what's complicated in all this?

Perhaps someone with a more subtle mind than mine can clarify it for me. But assuming one has the above information at hand, to me it seems to boil down to this: if we bomb (or even just threaten to bomb), they are more likely to starve. If we don't bomb (or threaten to bomb), they are less likely to starve. If we continue bombing, we are telling the innocent civilians who may starve — not thousands but millions of them — you just don't count. Compared to Washington's agenda, you are nothing.

And what is Washington's agenda?

Remarkably, the stated aim is to get bin Laden and to try him or perhaps just execute him ourselves. We could stop the bombing and have him tried in a third country, the Taliban has noted, but that's not acceptable. So for this minuscule gradation of difference, we are told that Washington is willing to risk the lives of millions of people.

Behind the rhetoric, the real goals appear to be to delegitimate international law, to establish that Washington will get its way regardless of impediments and that we can and will act unilaterally whenever it suits us — the technical term for which is to ensure that our threats remain "credible" — and to propel a long-term "war on terrorism" that will entrench the most reactionary policies in the United States and around the globe, and, along with all that, to terminate bin Laden and others.

Risking millions of people's lives for these aims is worse than doing it only for the minuscule gradation of trying bin Laden ourselves rather than having a third country do it, because the additional reasons are all grotesquely negative, supposing such calculus is even manageable by a sane mind.

When I was a kid and first learned about Nazi Germany, like many other kids, I asked how the German population could abide such horrors. I even wondered if maybe Germans were somehow genetically evil or amoral. I have long since understood that Germans weren't and aren't different from Brits or Americans or anyone else, though their circumstances were different, but for those who still don't understand mass subservience to vile crimes induced by structural processes of great power and breadth, I have to admit that I mostly just want to shout: Look around, dammit!

We live in a highly advanced country with means of communication that are virtually instantaneous and vastly superior to what the German populace had. We don't have a dictator and brownshirts threatening everyone who dissents. Dissent here can be somewhat unpleasant and may involve some sacrifice and risk, but the price is most often way less than incarceration, much less death.

That's fact one. Fact two is that our country is risking murdering a few million civilians in the next few months ... every serious commentator knows it, no serious commentator denies it ... and we are pursuing that genocidal path on the idiotic or grotesquely racist pretext that by so doing we are reducing terrorism in the world, even as we add millions to the tally of civilians currently terrorized for political purposes and simultaneously breed new hate and desperation that will yield still more terror in the future.

Does anyone remember "destroying the city to save it"? What's next? Terrorize the planet to rid it of terrorists?

For people of my generation, in the Vietnam War the U.S. killed roughly 2 million Vietnamese over years and years of horrible violation of the norms of justice, liberty, and plain humanity. The utterly incomprehensible truth is that the U.S. could attain that same level of massacre in the next few months, and, whether it happens or not, our leaders, our media moguls and commentators, in fact most of our "intelligentisia" are quite sanguine about doing so.

It is possible, with considerable effort, for the average person to discover that this "war" is potentially genocidal. One can easily get much more background, context, and analysis from the alternative media, but one can get that single insight, the possibility that genocidal calamity is imminent, even from the *New York Times, Washington Post,* or any major paper that one might read — if one digs deep into it and reads it very carefully, that is.

Of course, the fact that such information isn't prime time news in every outlet in the land reveals how supinely our media elevate obedience above truth. Our media pundits are seeing the aid agency and U.N. reports and calls for the bombing to be halted that I mentioned above. They are seeing stories about these in newspapers from Scotland to India, of course, but they are simply excluding the information from U.S. communications.

Yet even with this massive media obfuscation, which says volumes about our society, how hard is this war to comprehend, supposing one actually tries to comprehend it?

Shortly after September 11, a fifth-grader was quoted in the *New York Times* as asking, "If we strike back, aren't we doing the same thing that they did to us?"[5] This child wasn't a genius, just a normal elementary school student.

The real question is: why don't more of us see what the child instantly saw, even now, weeks later, with the horror in Afghanistan before our eyes?

Yes, a never-ending drum beat of patriotism proclaiming U.S. virtues and motives contributes to our blindness. Of course, accumulated confusions, augmented daily, cloud our understanding and push the sad facts of potential starvation out of our field of vision. And, yes, the human capacity for self-deception to avoid travail contributes, no doubt, to the process, as do anger and fear.

But I suspect most people's blindness is largely due to resignation. The key fact, I suspect, isn't that people don't know about the criminality of U.S. policies, though there is an element of that at work, especially in the more educated classes, to be sure. Even among those carefully groomed to be socially and politically ignorant — which is to say those who have a higher education — I think many people know at some broad level Washington's culpability for crimes. And of those who don't know, many don't in part because they are deceived, sure, but also in part because they are more or less actively avoiding this knowledge.

In my view, the key factor causing this avoidance isn't that people are sublimating comprehension to rationalizations due to a cowardly fear of the implications of dissent and wanting to run with the big crowd instead of against it. I think, instead, that people can find deep resources of courage if they think it will do some good. Witness those firefighters, average folks, running up the stairs of the World Trade Center.

Afterword

No, to me, the biggest impediment to dissenting is that people feel that they can't impact the situation in any useful way. If one has no positive hope, then it appears easiest and least painful, and even most productive, to toe the line and get on with life, trying to ignore the injustices perpetrated by one's country, or to give them an alibi, or even to claim them to be meritorious, while also trying to do what one can for one's kids and families, where we believe we can have an impact.

To admit the horror that our country is producing and to see the willingness of our elites and media to pursue and alibi that course (which is despicable whether the eventual horrors come to pass or not) seems to augur only alienation and tears. Here is one of many examples. A young woman recently sent me an e-mail that ended: "I've never had a huge amount of trust in governmental actions. But what I do know is that I have no control over anything. And all I can do is hope."

It follows that the task of those who understand the efficacy of dissent is not only to counter lies and rationalizations by calmly and soberly addressing all kinds of media-induced confusions that people have, but also to demonstrate to people their capacity to make a difference. We have to escort people, and sometimes ourselves, too, over the chasms of cynicism and doubt to the productivity of informed confidence.

Since September 11, we do not face, as some would claim, a transformed world turned upside down and inside out. Our DNA has not mutated. Our major social institutions are the same as they were yesterday, last week, and last year.

The main innovation in the events of September 11 is that major violence based in the third world hit people in the first world for the first time in modern history. But the problem of civilians being attacked is all too familiar. And all too often the perpetrator is us, or those we arm and empower, including even in this case, since bin Laden is a prime example of monstrous blowback. And now the problem is being replicated, writ ever larger, as if by a berserk Xerox machine.

What we have to do is precisely what we would want others to do: oppose barbaric policies with our words and deeds, arouse ever greater numbers of dissenters, and nurture ever greater commitment to dissent, until elites cannot sensibly believe that a "war on terrorism" will lead to anything but a population thoroughly fed up with and hostile to elites. People all over the world are embarking on this path. We should, too.

Notes

1 See Richard Falk, "Ends and Means: Defining a Just War," *The Nation* 273: 13 (October 29, 2001): 11–15. See also Stephen R. Shalom, "A 'Just War'? A Critique of Richard Falk," ZNet, October 21, 2001 (available on-line at http://www.zmag.org/shalomjustwar.htm).

2 See Alex Duval Smith, " 'Cease Air Strikes' So Aid Work Can Go On," *The Independent* (London), October 16, 2001, p. 4; Agence-France Presse, "US Military Food Drops a 'Catastrophe': UN Official," October 15, 2001; and Jonathan Fowler, "Expert: Food Drops Risk Future Aid," Associated Press, October 15, 2001.

3 Michelle Nichols and Paul Gallagher, "Bread Harder to Deliver Than Bombs," *The Scotsman,* October 8, 2001, p. 6.

4 Karen McVeigh, "Call Off Bombing, Plead Aid Agencies," *The Scotsman,* October 18, 2001, p. 4.

5 Eric Asimov, "After the Attacks: A Child's Version," *New York Times,* September 16, 2001, p. 1: 23.

Index

ABOUT THE AUTHOR

Michael Albert, a long-time activist, speaker, and writer, is editor of ZNet and co-editor and co-founder of *Z Magazine* (both on-line at http://www.zmag.org). He also co-founded South End Press and has written numerous books and articles. Albert developed along with Robin Hahnel the economic vision called "participatory economics," which challenges the foundations of economic theory and envisions a society based on participatory planning and council self-management. For more on participatory economics, visit the Parecon web site (http://www.parecon.org).

BOOKS AUTHORED AND EDITED BY MICHAEL ALBERT

What is to be Undone (Porter Sargent Press).

Unorthodox Marxism, with Robin Hahnel (South End Press).

Socialism Today and Tomorrow, with Robin Hahnel (South End Press).

Marxism and Socialist Theory, with Robin Hahnel (South End Press).

Michael Albert

Beyond Survival, with David Dellinger (South End Press).

Liberating Theory, with Lydia Sargent, Robin Hahnel, Mel King, Noam Chomsky, Leslie Cagan, and Holly Sklar (South End Press).

Looking Forward, with Robin Hahnel (South End Press).

The Political Economy of Participatory Economics, with Robin Hahnel (Princeton University Press)

A Quiet Revolution in Welfare Economics, with Robin Hahnel (Princeton University Press).

Stop the Killing Train (South End Press).

Thinking Forward (Arbeiter Ring).

Talking About a Revolution, interviews with Michael Albert, Noam Chomsky, Howard Zinn, Barbara Ehrenreich, bell hooks, Winona Laduke, Manning Marable, and Urvashi Vaid (South End Press).

Moving Forward (AK Press).

Parecon (Verso, forthcoming).

Radical Theory (Arbeiter Ring, forthcoming).

ABOUT THE PARTICIPATORY ECONOMICS PROJECT

Participatory economics (or parecon for short) is the name of a type of economy proposed as a desirable alternative to contemporary capitalism.

The underlying values that parecon seeks to implement are:

- equity
- solidarity
- diversity, and
- participatory self-management.

The main institutional vehicles to attain these ends are:

- council democracy
- balanced job complexes
- self-managed decision making
- remuneration according to effort and sacrifice, and
- participatory planning.

Michael Albert

The parecon vision is spelled out in a number of books:

Looking Forward (South End, 1991), the first full presentation of the model.

The Political Economy of Participatory Economics (Princeton, 1991), a more technical presentation primarily for economists.

Thinking Forward (Arbeiter Ring, 1997), which provides a course of lectures in thinking about economic vision, using parecon as a basis.

Moving Forward (AK Press, 2001), which includes argument for the vision, but also discussion of strategic program.

Parecon (Verso, forthcoming 2002), which gives a comprehensive account of the model, including treatment of diverse reasonable concerns.

Some of these titles are available on-line at the Parecon web site (http://www.parecon.org), which also includes numerous articles, interviews, instructional materials, links, and related information.

ABOUT ZNET

ZNet (http://www.zmag.org) is a web site sponsored by *Z Magazine* that prioritizes activism and movement involvement. Many of its components are interactive and focus on things people are doing or can do, and on providing information, vision, and strategy. A good example is the subsite devoted to the anti-corporate globalization movement.

Z Magazine articles usually go on-line from one to three months after publication, and about 1,000 Z articles are now available, plus many thousands of ZNet-originated and linked contents. You can view all articles by author or topic, as well as search them for key words.

In times of crisis, ZNet creates special sites to track busy topics. These range from "scandals" like Enron, to major left events like the Seattle demonstrations, and so on. Our War Terror pages provide our ongoing coverage and analysis of the so-called war on terrorism and related matters and give an example of a timely component focusing on a world crisis. Other watch sites include Colombia Watch, Alternative Media Watch, and Mideast Watch.

Michael Albert

People who wish to donate to Z can use the ZNet sustainer facilities. Premiums that users receive in thanks for their donations include daily sustainer commentaries, access to an on-line 'zine of commentaries, plus access to a forum system in which people can interact and ask various ZNet contributors like Noam Chomsky and Michael Albert questions and receive prompt replies.